Inclusive Leadership: From Awareness to Action

Dr. Ernest Gundling | Dr. Cheryl Williams

"*Inclusive Leadership* has achieved buzzword status: there's no shortage of noise out there on the topic. With this book, we finally have a truly useful resource that digs deeply into the thorny questions leaders must wrestle with, while providing highly practical advice on what leaders can actually do to create workplaces that are more inclusive, and that unleash massive organizational potential that too often lies dormant. This book will challenge you in all the best ways. Every leader who aspires to be more inclusive should read this book!"

> Jason D. Patent, Ph.D.
> Director, Robertson Center for Intercultural Leadership
> International House Berkeley

"Dr. Williams' experiences in business, academia and cultural anthropology shine though in this latest body of work. Having worked and partnered with Dr. Williams for more than 10 years, I find it wonderful that she is able to share her profound knowledge, experience, and wisdom. I continue to learn from her. My latest read from Dr. Williams and Dr. Gundling, **Inclusive Leadership: From Awareness to Action,** is spot on."

> Richard S. Spada, MA, PCC
> President and Principal Consultant, Aspire International, LLC, and former Global Executive Director, Diversity and Inclusion Center of Excellence, Novartis International

"*Inclusive Leadership* is a real contribution to organizations seeking to improve inclusion on a global scale, but also to the intercultural field as a whole. No one else is providing analysis that is so thorough and so practical."

> Dr. George Renwick
> President, Renwick & Associates

© 2019 Aperian Global

All rights reserved. No portion of this publication may be reproduced in any form without permission from Aperian Global. For permissions requests contact: contactus@aperianglobal.com.

CONTENTS

Acknowledgements | 1

1. Inclusive Leadership Trends | 5
2. Inclusive Leadership: Dealing with Difference | 25
3. Inclusive Behavior: Learning About Bias | 45
4. Unconscious Bias on a Global Team | 59
5. Inclusive Behaviors: Building Key Skills & Working Across Boundaries | 79
6. Inclusive Behaviors: Becoming a Champion & Getting Results | 107
7. Brain-Based Leadership: What's Missing? | 129
8. Regional Inclusion Challenges | 143
9. Inclusive Leadership Development | 163
10. Five Organizational Levers to Support Inclusion | 185

Endnotes | 219

Bibliography | 231

Resources | 237

About The Authors | 239

About Aperian Global | 241

Acknowledgements

Writing a book on the topic of inclusion creates a new appreciation for the value of a diverse set of contributors. The authors would like to acknowledge a number of people who have contributed their ideas and input during the writing process. Mercedes Martin, Theresa Kneebone, Pamela Leri, Ashley Coombs, Mike Greto, Adwoa Osei, Simone-Eva Redrupp, Morten Skov-Carlsen, Anthony Greco, Jason Overton, Jason Patent, and Ebenezer Amuasi all provided valuable comments on the manuscript along the way. Thanks to each of them and to many other colleagues at Aperian and in our field for their insights, advice, and dedication to a shared purpose.

Our wonderful, hard-working book production team of Sarah Cincotta, Nicole Ury, Tessah Clark, and Michelle Mascarenhas has seen this complex project through from start to finish. We appreciate their persistence, creativity, positive energy, and faith that we would eventually get this project done! It's been a pleasure to work with each of them, and special thanks to Michelle for her work on formatting and graphics. Kay Jones has been a disciplined and systematic editor, helping us to rein in our sometimes ungrammatical enthusiasm for this topic with both humor and concrete support in clarifying our intended message.

Dozens of clients and colleagues in the field have also provided various forms of input, encouragement, and opportunities for direct contact with current inclusive leadership challenges. We have mostly omitted reference to specific individuals and organizations out of respect for confidentiality, but would like to express our deep appreciation nonetheless. It has been our pleasure and privilege to work with them in every region mentioned in the book: Europe, the Middle East, sub-Saharan Africa, Asia-Pacific, and North and South America.

Finally, we are grateful for the patience, persistence, and encouragement of family members, especially Kacey and Kenny, who watched us wrestle with the writing process and how to bring the practice of inclusion to life in our own work by incorporating several rounds of feedback and commentary. The sharpest criticisms were often the ones that resulted in the greatest improvements to our original draft, but we also took a lot more time on this project than originally promised.

In addition to the many people who have contributed already, the authors welcome feedback, updates, and examples from readers. Feel free to reach out to us and provide your comments at **contactus@aperianglobal.com**. Although we can't promise to incorporate every contribution in future revisions given the extremely wide range of views on the topic of inclusive leadership, we will read every comment and consider carefully the views that you share with us.

> Against a background of rapid, unprecedented change on a global scale, inclusion is now a requirement for continued relevance in most industries.

CHAPTER ONE

Inclusive Leadership Trends

The practice of inclusion is relevant to everyone, particularly those in leadership roles. Growing a business requires opening new markets and hiring employees in other countries. Venture capitalists now encourage start-ups to launch with multicultural leadership teams—this can help them to scale rapidly, manage costs, and stay ahead of global competitors. Immigration and demographic changes mean that many organizations are becoming more diverse at headquarters, not to mention in their regional hubs or key country markets.

Smart leaders have also come to realize that they must get beyond ideas that are fixed in their own heads but no longer match reality, if they ever did. Developing a "growth mindset"[1] requires them to question stereotypes and other outdated perceptions that can limit their ability to engage all employees, access new information, and respond to fresh trends.

Inclusion has the most powerful impact when it is not just an initiative, a corporate principle, or a required training program. There is increasing recognition that all employees—CEO's, new hires, middle managers, cafeteria workers—have a role to play in making inclusion an integral part of the organizational fabric. Inclusion is most viable when it is not the goal of a single department, or the passion of a particular executive, interest group, or category of people. It is not "mine" or "theirs," but "ours," and is linked to core values such as human dignity, freedom, opportunity, meritocracy, and pragmatism.

Truly inclusive organizations are easy to identify because they are buzzing with energy and creativity, and have a magnetic attraction for talented individuals from any background; however, there is not a simple program or recipe to move from here to there. We will provide a general roadmap and practical recommendations for individuals, teams, and organizations to become more inclusive.

Key Questions

In this book we address a growing set of questions we are hearing from executives in many organizations that are seeking to become more inclusive.

- *How can we **deal with differences** without increasing mutual grievances among employees?*

- *Is there a concise approach to understanding and addressing **unconscious bias**?*

- *What is the impact of increased inclusiveness on **team performance**?*

- *What **practical steps** can leaders and employees take **to become more inclusive**? Beyond becoming aware of unconscious bias, what else can people do?*

- *How can leaders serve as **champions and effective models** of inclusion?*

- *What are the value and limits of current **neuroscience-based approaches** to inclusion and diversity?*

- *Are inclusion challenges the same everywhere, or are there **differences across regions** such as Asia-Pacific, EMEA (Europe, Middle East, and Africa), or North America?*

- *How can inclusive leadership be incorporated into **leadership development** programs?*

- *What kinds of **organizational changes** are essential to support inclusion?*

- *Is it possible to **measure progress** toward a more inclusive work environment?*

Inclusion Trends

The field of inclusion and diversity has changed considerably over time, and there is wide disparity among organizations. Some are still seeking to build a baseline awareness, while others have moved on to broader change initiatives. Before considering how leaders can contribute to an inclusive organizational culture, it is important to take stock of the current inclusion landscape. In our work we have encountered five major inclusion trends.

 Awareness to Action

The concept of unconscious bias has gained widespread acceptance, in part because research now suggests that rather than being a personal character defect, bias is a common human phenomenon—we all hold biases of varying types and degrees. Bias is now seen as being linked with the habits, or default shortcuts, that the human brain takes to ensure that attention and energy are used efficiently. Although most leaders working in diverse environments recognize that it is important to become aware of biases that shape exclusionary actions, many efforts to unwind such biases have become mired in complex terminology and finger-pointing. "Bias fatigue" may set in when people hear long lists of possible biases that are difficult to grasp and retain, while some individuals or groups feel that they are being singled out for blame. The concept of unconscious bias seems to entail a kind of infinite regress because unconscious biases are inexhaustible and must be continually revisited. There is a growing trend to tie awareness to action—leaders and employees not only face the challenge of how to think inclusively, but how to act in more inclusive ways as well.

Another way to address bias is through engaging in deliberate acts of inclusion. Psychological research tells us that action can shape attitudes, just as the reverse is also true.[2] New behaviors, however awkward they might feel at first, stimulate the development of related mental patterns that in turn provide further support for such behaviors. Insights quickly dissipate without follow-up actions, but a **mutually reinforcing cycle of insight and action** can become a powerful personal and organizational change agent. Although some might claim that focusing on inclusive action is a way to avoid talking about unconscious bias, it may have the opposite effect by generating experiences that make the presence of bias and the need to address it more tangible.

> **There is a growing trend to tie awareness to action—leaders and employees not only face the challenge of how to think inclusively, but also how to act in more inclusive ways as well.**

Over the past decade it has also become common to reverse the term, "Diversity and Inclusion," to "Inclusion and Diversity," reflecting the aspiration to move beyond awareness of differences to cultivating inclusive behaviors across the workforce over time (although some still argue that diversity logically comes before inclusion). Experts and practitioners in this field have made great strides in defining what inclusive behaviors look like, and **how leaders can evolve from basic awareness of unconscious bias to becoming workplace champions and role models.**[3]

Digitalization and Demographics

Powerful social currents are likely to keep driving urgent calls for more inclusive leadership. An approach favored by some executives has been to hunker down and wait for the inclusion movement to blow over and to be replaced by some other faddish trend. Others make a show of supporting initiatives while going through the motions of minimal compliance, with little enthusiasm for anything further. But both technological innovation and demographic trends make such a head-in-the-sand approach unrealistic.

Digital technologies connect people across oceans, mountains, and deserts, and are able to magnify negative or positive interactions almost instantly; twice as many people on the planet are connected to the internet now as there were a decade ago, with rapidly increasing bandwidth. A simultaneous transformation is occurring in the location of future customers, employees, suppliers, and fast-growth markets. Several key underlying demographic changes are not only roiling global markets, but also transforming the headquarters operations of almost every major multinational.

- *Population Growth*: *We've nearly tripled the planet's population* in the last seventy years, from 2.5 billion to over 7 billion, and this has affected every region of the world. Almost all of this explosive population growth is occurring in emerging markets,[4] with billions more people on the way over the rest of this century to reach the earth's projected peak population of 9 to 11 billion. 90% of the world's children under the age of 15 currently live outside of developed economies in Europe, North America, and Japan.

  Differences in birth rates are leading to major changes both between and within countries. The highest birth rates globally are in sub-Saharan Africa (e.g., Niger, Uganda, Zambia) and in South Asia, with the lowest rates being in northeast Asia and in Europe (e.g., Taiwan, Japan, Germany, Italy). To provide an illustration of how stark these contrasts are, in a recent year approximately the same number of babies were born in Niger, with a population of 21 million, as in Japan, with a population of 126 million. In the U.S., although non-Hispanic whites currently comprise two-thirds of the nationwide population, this ratio is predicted to decline to less than half of the overall country population in 2050 due to comparatively low birth rates, in spite of a recent decline in minority births.

- *Urbanization and the Middle Class*: *The expansion of new cities is driving two-thirds of the world's GDP growth*, with millions of people moving to cities each month from rural areas in search of new opportunities. Hundreds of additional cities will be required to house all of these people, and in addition, the citizens of each new city will need to purchase manufactured goods, transportation, food, and energy. Many of these people are still living in terrible poverty. At the same time, there is a huge and rapidly growing new urban middle class of consumers that will soon number a billion people or more. Its members in Asia, Africa, the Middle East, and South America desire many of the products and services enjoyed by residents of the current high-consumption markets.

- ***International Migration***: *Migration across national borders has increased by almost 50% since the year 2000*, with the primary flow of people moving to high-income countries. Millions of people emigrate every year to escape from poverty, conflict, or natural disasters. A United Nations study notes that the number of migrants as a fraction of the population residing in high-income countries has risen from under 10% to almost 15% on average. Three-quarters of these migrants are of working age, and they normally seek to join the workforce as quickly as possible in their new locations.[5]

 ## Global Principles, Local Knowledge

More than ten years ago we published *Global Diversity: Winning Customers and Engaging Employees within World Markets*. In that book we pointed out that it is **essential to view diversity through a local lens**, exploring this topic in eight countries: China, India, Egypt, Mexico, Japan, Russia, the U.K., and the U.S. Organizations had been reporting that their attempts to roll out global inclusion initiatives were falling flat or generating unanticipated resistance. The primary reason for such failed efforts was that they were based on headquarters' perspectives and experiences, and

the concepts and practices they conveyed often did not resonate with local employees and their issues.

While some organizations have learned from earlier trials and are working hard to integrate the priorities of both headquarters and regional markets, others have continued to discover the hard way that **imposing one set of culturally-based assumptions on employees and customers elsewhere is a dependable recipe for failure**, and an ironic violation of vital inclusion principles. Even when an initiative is supported with the best of intentions, negative outcomes are especially likely when it is deeply rooted in the original home country's distinctive history and business environment. More successful efforts usually highlight **a short list of core principles while at the same time leaving room for adaptation and interpretation based on local circumstances**. Beyond national cultural orientations, it is essential to understand **"cultures within cultures,"** or the astonishing diversity that exists within each country as well.

Clifford Geertz, renowned for his meticulous anthropological field work and his respect for the cultures he encountered, emphasized the value of "thick description"—that is, knowing a place well enough to grasp how people understand themselves and their own world. He asserts:

> *The next necessary thing...is neither the construction of a universal Esperanto-like culture...nor the invention of some vast technology of human management. It is to enlarge the possibility of intelligible discourse between people quite different from one another in interest, outlook, wealth, and power, and yet contained in a world where tumbled as they are into endless connection, it is increasingly difficult to get out of each other's way.*[6]

What Geertz is saying is important for practical businesspeople as well as for academicians to consider: **deep mutual understanding is an essential basis for meaningful conversation**. For better or worse, the world's cultures appear to be diverging in some respects just as they may be converging in others. If anything, for example, global trends toward democratic government and science-based reasoning once thought to be inexorable have slowed or even reversed. Mutually hostile autocracies, defined along ethnic and tribal lines, now commonly claim to have characteristics that make them superior to their neighbors. Meanwhile, fundamentalism, blossoming under a variety of lethal banners, looks to literal interpretations of sacred texts rather than to science for policy guidelines.

Compliance Challenges (Again)

Progress in blending global inclusion principles with local knowledge has been accompanied by **a renewed emphasis on compliance challenges**. Many of these have come as a painful surprise even to global firms proud of their brands and their prior image as progressive employers. Inclusion experts once predicted an enlightened advance from legal compliance efforts to more sophisticated organizational processes designed to leverage diversity for product innovation, employee engagement, or new market entry. However, with increasing political polarization in many locations concerning hot-button issues such as terrorism, immigration, and gaps between rich and poor—often fueled by inflammatory rhetoric—compliance has become, if anything, more important than ever.

For example, major commercial and academic institutions in the U.S., including Uber, Google, and Harvard University, have been hit with charges of discrimination based on race, gender, or political views, taking them back to basic compliance measures such as conducting mandatory training and establishing standard grievance processes. Accusations of sexual harassment are reported regularly in the news. Corporate leaders have discovered that workplace actions or even tweets of individual employees or of CEOs themselves can quickly go viral and spark legal and public relations firestorms that incur enormous costs.

Compliance requirements have continued to be a corporate priority for other reasons as well. A number of European countries, including Norway, France, Germany, Spain, Italy, and the Netherlands have mandated quotas for public companies to have a minimum representation of women on their boards—companies that fail to comply with these quotas risk penalties such as the nullification of existing boards. Meanwhile, strict European privacy laws have set off a new compliance scramble by companies worldwide that do business with European counterparts and customers. Google has already been fined $57 million by France's data protection agency for alleged failure to comply with the EU's General Data Protection Regulation (GDPR).[7] In addition to avoiding discrimination against individuals or groups based on specific characteristics, now organizations must institute procedures to protect the privacy of their unique data and preferences expressed online. Inclusiveness in the form of personal data collection may be defined as intrusive, and it is necessary for internet service providers to preserve a clear and simple right to "opt out."

So at the same time that inclusion has become a much more universal topic, with global initiatives now being driven by companies based in EMEA and Asia Pacific as well as North America, results have been mixed. **"Two steps forward and one step back" and the legal equivalent of "whack-a-mole"** seem to be common patterns for companies that seek to move beyond focusing primarily on compliance.

Competitive Advantage

Some early approaches to "diversity" involved keeping the topic in a corner removed from the real business, while checking compliance boxes provided by corporate counsel and thereby limiting exposure to risk—but this approach has turned out to be inadequate even for risk mitigation. In recent years, an expanding body of research has more fully defined the business case for inclusion, with tangible evidence for the competitive advantage created by inclusive work environments. Claims regarding the business benefits of inclusion are still challenged and have many silent doubters: "How is an inclusion initiative going to help me meet my sales goals?" The research data connecting inclusion with significant business benefits do generally demonstrate correlation rather than direct causality, but this evidence coupled with the demographic trends outlined previously has become increasingly compelling.

Against a background of rapid, unprecedented change on a global scale, **inclusion is now a requirement for continued relevance** in most industries. No matter where a company is headquartered, promising growth market opportunities are often situated in distant and relatively unfamiliar places. McKinsey predicts that as the center of the global economy continues to shift, nearly half of Fortune 500 companies will be headquartered in emerging markets by 2025—up from just 5% percent in 2000.[8]

Specific inclusion benefits cited in various studies are innovation, success in growth markets, better business outcomes, and the acquisition and retention of top talent worldwide. Such positive outcomes are not an automatic result of bringing different people together, of course, but are best achieved through targeted inclusive actions that harness the forces of "divergence" and "convergence" in diverse workplaces. Here are sample statistics that affirm the business case for both diversity and inclusion:

The Business Case: Sample Statistics

- Companies with above-average diversity on their management teams reported innovation revenue that was 19 percentage points higher and EBIT margins that were 9% higher than companies with below-average leadership diversity.[9]

- Employees of firms with diverse leadership teams are 45% more likely to report a growth in market share over the previous year, and 70% likelier to report that the firm captured a new market.[10]

- Organizations with inclusive work cultures are twice as likely to exceed their financial targets.[11]

- Companies with ethnically diverse leadership teams are 33% more likely to outperform their competitors.[12]

- Two-thirds of job seekers consider a company's diversity when making decisions about where to work.[13]

- Employees at companies with high levels of both diversity and inclusion report a 12% higher level of discretionary effort, and a 19% higher level of intent to stay with their current organization (discretionary effort and retention are the two primary indicators of employee engagement); they also report significantly greater team collaboration and commitment.[14]

- Women will control 75% of discretionary spending worldwide by 2028.[15]

Leaders still not persuaded by such research will probably see the wisdom in avoiding the expensive compliance disasters described previously; in fact, this is a topic of quiet discussion in many boardrooms. Costs of settlements and legal defense fees for a single incident—not to mention the distractions that crisis management poses for those who should be running the business—can easily run into tens of millions of dollars, and other expenses may be incurred through boycotts, mandatory training, government-imposed fines, damage to brand reputation, and so on. Charges of anti-Semitism, anti-gay bias, discrimination based on race, or inequitable treatment of new fathers have been made in recent years against companies and industries as disparate as Delta Airlines, the Italian pasta maker Barilla, the Al Jazeera news network, and Estée Lauder, the French cosmetics giant. Many organizations have dozens if not hundreds of such pending claims that they are facing simultaneously, with in-house legal staff and/or external counsel (billing in 15 minute increments), dedicated to defending them.

After an alleged racial discrimination incident in a Philadelphia store, for instance, Starbucks lost an estimated $12 million in sales when it shut down all of its U.S. stores for an afternoon to put 175,000 employees through racial-bias training. The full cost of this single incident was probably double or triple the reported sales loss if other expenses are tallied: legal counsel, public relations, training delivery, employee wages, and the confidential settlement payment made to the individuals involved. In a separate event, an engineer formerly employed at Lockheed Martin charged the company with age discrimination after he was laid off at age 66, and was awarded a $51 million settlement. Regulatory sanctions or class-action suits can be even more expensive than the costs for a specific incident, and some lead to public charges against executives. Possible compliance issues vary from country to country; they may be based on strict labor and union rules as well as laws that forbid discrimination against protected classes. Some governments make a practice of cracking down on relatively minor violations by foreign companies as an example to domestic firms, and also to give their local players a bit of an edge—all the more reason to avert legal or regulatory claims proactively by creating an inclusive organizational culture in addition to following the letter of the law.

Whether inclusion efforts are ultimately driven by the promise of better business results or implemented as a risk mitigation strategy, the value of a significant investment in them is clear, as the potential rewards and costs can both affect an organization's ability to compete in the global marketplace.

Figure 1.1: Inclusion Trends

1. Awareness to Action
2. Digitalization and Demographics
3. Global Principles, Local Knowledge
4. Compliance Challenges (Again)
5. Competitive Advantage

Organizational Vitality

On a more qualitative level, what is at stake with inclusive leadership is nothing less than organizational vitality. Institutions generally have a center and spokes, as does any wheel. There are myriad variations in organizational structure, and some are designed to have multiple centers, but they all need a healthy flow of ideas and information among people and places. Organizations with a one-sided flow of information, whether this is top-down within the same office or between headquarters and subsidiaries, are likely to stagnate and fail to meet changing environmental circumstances. John Kotter, one of the best-known scholars of leadership and change management, emphasizes that a strong organizational culture can be a blessing or a curse—a powerful asset so long as it is suited to the surrounding marketplace, but a fatal flaw when there is no longer a match between this culture and its environment.[16]

Unhealthy organizations, including dictatorships as well as corporate autocracies, find **scapegoats**, singling out individuals—usually those who can be labeled as different in some way based on their appearance or their ideas—to blame for poor performance results; these people are then chastised and cast out while the perpetrators claim the problem is solved. But sooner or later, underlying issues that have not been addressed resurface, and then the hunt is on again for a new scapegoat. This social pattern—which is found in every civilization and even in ancient societies—commonly leads to a recurring cycle of exclusion and underperformance, with a spiraling descent into ruin.

Autocratic leaders are seldom inclined to embrace inclusion and diversity, and there is nothing inevitable about social change in a dictatorship other than lethal battles for succession. Leaders may indeed decide that it is politically expedient to blame, persecute, or expel residents who appear different or who fail to sing a one-party refrain with sufficient gusto. Pitting "them" against "us" is a convenient way to distract national or corporate citizens from problems that are actually self-created. More inclusive forms of governance, on the other hand, must bridge divergent interests, however imperfectly, to create a more productive and vibrant union.

Rather than blaming others who are different and casting them out as scapegoats, inclusive leaders connect people at various levels and locations. They serve as catalysts for collaborative problem-solving, keeping the organization's culture current with the times while seeing themselves clearly enough in the mirror to take responsibility for problems that they themselves have caused. Individuals who might previously have been candidates to become **scapegoats may turn out to be innovators, inspirational trend-setters, and future leaders.**

Inclusive Behaviors: Five Developmental Stages

So how can individuals and organizations surmount bias and realize the full benefits of inclusion—both at home and on a global scale—while avoiding the temptations of simple yet ultimately destructive solutions such as scapegoating? The recent emphasis on coupling awareness with action has also driven a **move from learning events to a learning journey**. Building new patterns of behavior strong enough to counteract entrenched habits and even primal, atavistic impulses requires creating a shared language, multiple touch points, and various forms of reinforcement.

The ultimate goal for many current inclusion champions is to build a transformative, high-performance organizational culture that also serves as a greenhouse for developing inclusive leaders. Inclusion is neither a cure-all for every business problem nor the ticket to a socialist utopia. It will not erase historical injustices, and it cannot eliminate distinctions between people based on power, privilege, or hierarchy. Inclusive leaders, however, can seize the possibilities that are inherent in the present to work toward a better future that offers equal opportunities to all, regardless of their background.

Figure 1.2 outlines a progression that we often see in inclusive leaders and their organizations. These five stages are not strictly sequential but flourish in mutually reinforcing cycles. Each stage creates a foundation for those that follow—"Building Key Skills," for example, is a gateway to "Becoming a Champion"—and yet each also remains an ongoing project, including "Learning About Bias." Leaders are never *done* with the work of inclusion and able to cross this item off their task lists, but they can make enormous changes over time, especially when they exert steady efforts to practice inclusion on a daily basis. The chapters that follow provide a roadmap for aspiring inclusive leaders to make every one of these stages come alive, and to move from awareness to action.

Chapter Overview

The chapters in this book address the questions about inclusive leadership and the trends previously mentioned. We also incorporate newer themes such as intersectionality, third-culture kids, and cultural neuroscience, along with data from empirical studies on global leadership. Our primary focus is on individual development; the book outlines key organizational levers for change as well. Here is a brief description of each chapter:

Figure 1.2: Five Stages of Inclusion

Learning about Bias
How aware am I of my own biases, and how do I begin to learn about others who are different?

Building Key Skills
What critical baseline skills do I have for acting in a more inclusive way?

Working Across Boundaries
How successful am I in working with various aspects of diversity such as gender, generational, functional, cognitive, or cultural diversity?

Becoming a Champion
What does it mean to champion inclusion, and am I doing what it takes?

Getting Results
How well do I link inclusion to business results?

Chapter 1: Inclusive Leadership Trends
Describes an emerging set of questions about inclusive leadership along with major trends; outlines a five-stage developmental model for moving from exclusion to better workplace performance through inclusive leadership.

Chapter 2: Inclusive Leadership: Dealing with Difference
Covers the hazards and benefits of addressing differences in race, ethnicity, gender, function, culture, cognitive style, and other aspects of a diverse workforce, while providing a clear model for proactively leveraging differences.

Chapter 3: Inclusive Behavior: Learning About Bias
Examines the renewed urgency for inclusive practices in current workplaces and how organizational values are being tested; describes the simple and memorable CIAO model that defines four key types of unconscious bias using everyday examples; highlights empathy as the doorway to inclusive action.

Chapter 4: Unconscious Bias on a Global Team
Takes the concept of unconscious bias beyond the realm of individual awareness and examines how it can create a downward spiral of mistrust and underperformance in a diverse, dispersed team context unless proactively addressed by the team leader and the team as a whole.

Chapter 5: Inclusive Behaviors: Building Key Skills & Working Across Boundaries
Provides practical recommendations for cultivating key inclusion skills in areas such as mutual listening, feedback, meeting facilitation, and conflict resolution; challenges leaders to expand their inclusive actions to incorporate new and unfamiliar types of counterparts.

Chapter 6: Inclusive Behaviors: Becoming a Champion & Getting Results
Offers guidance for leaders on how to move beyond their immediate work teams and contribute to the broader organization as inclusion champions through either one-on-one interactions or process improvements; identifies specific means by which inclusive practices can be leveraged to create better performance results.

Chapter 7: Brain-Based Leadership: What's Missing?
Highlights the deficit of cultural knowledge in common neuroscience-based approaches to leadership development, as well as ways to address this by incorporating the findings of "cultural neuroscience."

Chapter 8: Regional Inclusion Challenges
Explores how to overcome inclusion obstacles that are common in various regions and countries, and how inclusion initiatives can begin to integrate global principles with local knowledge.

Chapter 9: Inclusive Leadership Development
Offers a diagnosis of why leadership development programs tend to fall short of their objectives due to fatal flaws such as headquarters-centrism and the "parade of professors"; spells out alternative practices based on global trends that provide current and future leaders with first-hand experience in the markets of the future along with a trusted network of global peers.

Chaper 10: Five Organizational Levers to Support Inclusion
Provides recommendations for how inclusive leaders and their organizations can build a culture of inclusion using five critical change levers: recruitment; executive engagement; coaching and mentoring; key performance indicators; and policy and process.

CHAPTER TWO

Inclusive Leadership: Dealing with Difference

How can we deal with differences without increasing mutual grievances among employees?

Inclusive leadership has increasingly come to blend issues previously considered to be either "cross-cultural" or aspects of "domestic diversity." Proponents and practitioners of this fused brand of inclusive leadership development have expressed fresh concerns about the potential hazards of overexposure to differences. Is examination of the full plethora of cultural, racial, ethnic, regional, linguistic, cognitive, and generational differences within a diverse multicultural work environment more likely to lead to deep understanding and alignment, or to fuel a heightened sense of separation and grievance?

> The empathy, perspective, and flexibility developed through crucible experiences foster a strong sense of kinship and future possibility across an organization.

Learning modalities that produce a sense of mild discomfort, followed by a quick reintegration to consolidate learnings and restore comfort, comprise a classic instructional methodology. However, diverse groups can be explosive if "discomfort" ignites anger or resentment. Comments from program participants such as, **"You will never understand my life experience,"** or **"I feel like I'm being blamed for something I didn't do"** are the bane of facilitators, and may escalate into serious conflicts if not expertly handled. **Better to highlight common organizational objectives and set aside differences, some would say,** including both educators and others informed by neuroscience. They advocate making learners a bit uncomfortable so their brains are stimulated to make new neural connections and to retain what they have learned, but prefer not to take people very far out of their comfort zones, often finding solace in the dubious proposition that differences are gradually melting away amidst the global deluge of social media.

However, **such a cautious approach is insufficient to cultivate leaders who are mature, seasoned, and steeped in global experience.** The doctrine of safe and cheerful incrementalism focuses on common goals, shared language, and experiences of mild to moderate discomfort—such techniques are all useful in building awareness and skills for everyday use. Yet this approach brings with it risks of its own, including papering over real differences, muffling important voices that seek to be heard in languages of their own, and shaping leaders who are oblivious to the rigors and potential rewards of life on the edges of their organizational worlds.

It is better to focus on what we have in common.

Cultures are converging in the digital age.

"I want our leaders to have a real experience of what it is like to be excluded," some learning professionals say, and their instincts are well-founded. **Both research and practical experience support the value of "crucible" experiences that take leaders through the fire of intense trials** to forge new and creative approaches to their work. Learning journeys that include mild discomfort and incremental learning can be part of this approach, but are normally insufficient to produce profound personal transformation unless they involve rigorous, gut-wrenching experiences.

Differences that Divide

In the expanding world of training on diversity and inclusion, now often mandated by companies and even governments, there are many ways to alienate participants rather than to facilitate deep conversation and mutual learning. In addition to the involuntary aspect of certain programs that is off-putting from the start, terminology such as **"unearned advantage,"** which may make sense in an academic context, is perceived as offensive by some would-be learners. Few employees who have been in their jobs for several years or more, especially if they have begun to take on leadership roles, would feel that their roles and responsibilities, let alone their salaries, are unearned. "I have worked hard to get where I am," most people would claim. Even leaders born with the proverbial silver spoon in their mouths tend to develop impervious rationales for why they have earned their places in the organizational hierarchy. **Perceived questioning of a person's work ethic and accomplishments is more likely to produce resistance and even rage rather than an open mind and heart.**

Likewise, "targets" for the hiring and promotion of minorities and women sometimes begin to sound like **quotas**—certain types of which are in fact legal in countries such as India and Canada—and engender a spoken or unspoken sense of unfairness. Correcting a historical imbalance doesn't necessarily feel right in the present moment to employees who believe that they have been passed over in favor of other people who seem less qualified, although this may be absolutely justified in the eyes of those who want to build a more equitable future.

As pointed out in Chapter 1, there is also an increasing sense of unconscious bias fatigue in many organizations. The list of potential biases, now well over a hundred and continuing to grow, seems elusive and impossible to master. These biases are by definition unconscious to begin with; **dealing with subtle biases is like the legendary task of Sisyphus to roll a rock uphill only to have it come rolling down again**. How can leaders possibly remember a functional list of biases let alone apply them in their daily work? Who wants to be blamed and yet feel that there is no way to emerge from a cycle of attempted redress and fresh complaints?

At worst, a clumsy focus on differences creates a shared climate of **hypersensitivity** and drives groups of people apart with a heightened sense of mutual injustice. These tribal divisions can be reinforced by stereotypes and labels that paint the other tribe with broad, threatening brushstrokes. Far from finding common organizational goals, the new focus becomes **payback** to right supposed wrongs, and a conviction that the **others will never "get it."** Sociopolitical factors can make diverse groups even more combustible, with extreme political viewpoints and social commentary providing the tinder for heated emotional exchanges and little real listening.

Coffee Clash

In the office break room two employees were discussing recent news over coffee. They shared the same political views and were nodding in agreement with each other. Another employee

> *wandered in and overheard their conversation. After listening quietly for a couple of minutes he began to question the two colleagues sitting at the table, and a difference of opinion quickly emerged. As the conversation continued, the tone started to become more heated. A fourth person entered the room, and she began to challenge the first two as well. It became clear that the four people in the room had voted for different political candidates and were receiving their news from different, conflicting sources. There were racial and ethnic differences in the group as well. In fact, there was little that the members of this group had in common besides working for the same organization in the same location and taking a break at the same time. Referring to the gaps between them, one person said in frustration, "You just don't get it, and I'm not sure you ever will." The person to whom the comment was directed replied, "I don't think you understand me very well either," resulting in a very uncomfortable standoff. After a pause, the last person to enter the room commented, "It's a free country. We don't have to agree, or to embrace everything about each other all the time. Don't we just want to create a place where we can all do our best to contribute?" With this statement the atmosphere of the room shifted. What had seemed like a long and potentially dangerous conversation only lasted for ten minutes, and everyone soon headed back to work.*

From a broad social and historical viewpoint, **the ideology behind "celebrating diversity" is in fact much less universal than its proponents commonly recognize.** Many countries, based on their own historical experiences, energetically downplay or suppress diversity in various forms—ethnic, religious, or linguistic, for example—regarding it as a potential source of chaos and division rather than an asset.

Minority populations are routinely persecuted, expelled, or exterminated on the grounds that they are troublemakers (one example is Myanmar's lethal treatment of its Rohingya minority). A more superficially benevolent tactic is to endorse and publicize beautiful costumes and folk dances, while at the same time ruthlessly crushing any sign of actual resistance to those in power, and smothering the charming locals with administrators, immigrants, and police supervision. Forced assimilation is not just a relic of unenlightened eras of the past, but a current reality in some countries where leaders prefer to dilute or erase differences rather than to embrace them.

Figure 2.1: "You don't get it."

Differences that Strengthen

So why encourage open exploration of real differences when this could lead to trouble? **Why not simply avoid differences or at most consider them only in small, safe doses if they can take us down a dark and divisive path?** What is it about experiencing difference that is so crucial for aspiring leaders?

Although exposure to difference is in fact challenging and potentially hazardous, the most successful global leaders frequently report that their **"fish out of water" experience** in a new country, business, or function—and the struggles and failures that came along with it—**was their most formative career phase**. Research from multiple sources supports this assertion, highlighting the effects of such experiences in shaping key leadership capabilities.

The Corporate Executive Board (CEB), for instance, in one of the largest empirical studies ever carried out on the topic of global leadership development, with more than 11,000 survey respondents across many companies and industries, concludes that passage through demanding "crucible" experiences is closely correlated with the ability of leaders to exert the critical skill of influence. They recommend that "organizations should focus on providing leaders with development experiences that push them outside of their comfort zones and in unfamiliar environments." Such experiences include tackling new roles outside of one's functional area of expertise, working in a new market, or running a new business. They can also consist of leading the turnaround of an underperforming project or team, or managing a critical project on a fast cycle. **The most effective leadership development experiences of all,** according to the CEB study, **are "crucible experiences that occur in an international context."**[1]

Figure 2.2: "Fish Out of Water"

In a similar vein, INSEAD researcher William Maddux has found a **strong correlation between living abroad and increased creativity**. Study participants who had lived abroad scored significantly higher on an established test of creativity than did others without this experience, and the longer people had lived abroad, the higher they scored. Shorter-term travel abroad did not produce the same effect:

> *We don't find a positive correlation with travel abroad and creativity... The more people had adapted while they were abroad, the more creative they were... Not only does the time matter, which can explain why living abroad matters and not traveling abroad, but also the psychological transformation that you might go through while you are abroad.*

Furthermore, Maddux notes, even "priming" participants to remember their fish-out-of-water experiences in other countries led to significantly more creative responses than when participants were not primed in the same way. He cites a similarly strong correlation between time spent living abroad and entrepreneurial activity. Building barriers between cultures, he concludes, runs counter to innovation.[2]

Crucible experiences, although they can be more or less effectively supported, are not consistently pleasant or contained. Some careers do not survive or are sidetracked by this experience, and family solidarity is often tested. **According to seasoned leaders, the underlying reason why a crucible of some kind was so vital to their development is that it forced them to make a wrenching reassessment of previous patterns of success that had turned out to be dysfunctional in their new environment**. Proud and previously successful people taste real failure, perhaps for the first time in their lives, learn humility, and scramble to understand their new context and how to become effective in it. They must make new personal connections, ask for help, question fundamental assumptions, and try novel strategies and tactics. "Fall down seven times and get up eight" is an expression for the resilience that such leaders discover and come to value along the way. By tasting such adversity they also learn to empathize with others who are going through struggles of their own, including colleagues from very different walks of life.

These difficult and even excruciating lessons are unlikely to occur through other increasingly trendy forms of what some learning and development professionals are now calling "micro-," "bite-sized," or even "snack-sized" learning, which offers carefully curated yet ultimately minor insights. By way of contrast, one former expatriate reported, "My whole team in our Bangkok office quit within my first six months as their leader because they could not accept my more direct, aggressive, and results-oriented leadership style." This was a riveting crisis that challenged his sense of competence and personal efficacy, and the leader who went through this painful process wound up hiring a new team, altered his style to become more effective at managing and coaching employees in his new context, and now heads up a major function back at headquarters for a Fortune 100 company. "The most effective managers often suffer the most severe culture shock," notes Nancy Adler, one of the most respected scholars of expatriate effectiveness.[3]

In addition to a large body of empirical research, myths and legends from various cultural settings tell us that great leaders build wisdom and courage by embarking on journeys, encountering many obstacles, and ultimately facing existential, fire-breathing threats. **No mythical hero slays a tame, carefully curated dragon**. Sacred texts from many traditions share similar lessons. The patriarch Moses, who is recognized by Judaism, Christianity, and Islam, lived through a lengthy exile in Egypt before starting the journey back to the Promised Land. He named his son Gershom, sometimes translated as "exile," commemorating the experience of being a **"stranger in a strange land."**[4] Moses became a stronger and more capable leader through the trials he encountered during a life in exile.

Figure 2.3: The Crucible Experience

Distilling Difference

There is an alternative to the flight to safe but narrow common goals, or experiences of difference that only heighten conflicts and divisions. As the Corporate Executive Board study suggests, a crucible experience can take on a variety of forms, and it is not essential to send every employee on a lengthy assignment abroad for them to encounter and learn from real differences. Warren Bennis defines this experience as "a trial and a test, a point of deep self-reflection that forced (leaders) to question who they were and what mattered to them"; he notes that crucibles appear in many forms that may also involve encounters with prejudice at home as well as abroad, working with a demanding mentor, or handling a crisis.[5] Targeted career experiences include moves to different functions, business units, or particularly challenging projects. The mythical journeys upon which heroes used to embark are now available down the hallways of many domestic workplaces, which hold myriad people and voices from around the world. These can be a rich source of new experiences and perspectives for individuals who seek to learn.

Home is Not Homogeneous

Exclusion is a universal human phenomenon, and there are likely to be those in our everyday environments who are confronting this experience firsthand.

Feedback for Latisha

Latisha is in her first year on the job in the marketing department at a major U.S. manufacturing firm. She entered as a mid-career hire, having specialized in marketing in school and at her previous company. She likes her current employer and has been working hard to continue building her professional career, but has been frustrated by the lack of feedback thus far from her manager. This manager seems to spend a lot more time talking and laughing with other team members, and Latisha has also heard her making comments and offering advice to them on their reports and presentations.

Inspired by a recent "Growth Mindset" training event put on by her company that encouraged employees to reach out and request feedback, Latisha decided to ask directly for the feedback that she hadn't been receiving. Normally a shy person, she mustered the courage to ask her manager: "Do you have any feedback for me? I'd really like to know what I can do better." After a few seconds of reflection, her manager responded, "Well, one thing you could do is to smile more. You need to make the people around you feel more comfortable."

Latisha was amazed and disappointed by this response, as it seemed so far from her own self-image. Her mind was full of thoughts that she didn't want to say out loud to her manager for fear of

> *putting a good job at risk. "Oh, so just because I'm trying to put on a serious professional face at work you're afraid of some angry black woman stereotype that you have in your mind and you want me to smile more? Don't you know that my name actually means 'joy'? What about some concrete feedback on the quality of my work or the ideas I've been raising at meetings? I've already been feeling like I can't bring my whole best self to work, and now you're telling me to paste on a pretty smile? If you're uncomfortable with me, is that my responsibility or yours? My family and friends, who have always worked in blue collar jobs, say that they hardly recognize me when I dress up for work, and now you tell me that you're not comfortable with me here on the job! I feel like I'm not black enough for my family, and not white enough to be working here. Where does that leave me?"*

Latisha's manager may never hear her unvoiced thoughts, and perhaps she would be disappointed but also a bit relieved when Latisha leaves for another job. But what if she did get to know her better and learn to understand her background, her concerns, her challenges, and her potential? Wouldn't this be stepping into a different world for her as well? Not only could Latisha benefit from feedback that would actually help her to improve her performance on the job, but the manager could overcome stereotypical images and unfounded fears that may be influencing her own perceptions, while learning to work more effectively with a valuable employee. There are dragons for this team leader to slay in her own mind, and she doesn't need to journey far to encounter them.

> ## Why leave behind the seat that exists in your home and go aimlessly off to the dusty realms of other lands?

Accelerated Learning

While crucible career experiences are not guaranteed to be safe, and there are bound to be casualties along the way, the insights they produce are life-changing rather than tepid, and the leaders who emerge are far more ready to tackle today's swirling VUCA forces: volatility, uncertainty, change, and ambiguity.

Crucible experiences, along with structured learning and development, can all be supported to produce positive results at an accelerated pace with the help of skilled managers, facilitators, coaches, and mentors. Here are some common principles:

- Equip the learner with **baseline skills** for reserving judgment and engaging in proactive inquiry when encountering unexpected differences.

- Use tools and techniques to encourage and reinforce **self-awareness** of one's psychological and cultural background.

- Provide periodic opportunities for structured **orientation, reflection, and course correction**.

- Enable **network-building** among learners going through similar experiences who can share key learnings with each other and provide mutual support.

- Bring learners into contact with **mentors and coaches** who help them make sense of their experiences and support them as they experiment with new approaches.

Structured learning programs augment on-the-job encounters with difference by offering exposure to a diverse mix of people and ideas. They ideally feature **a wide array of viewpoints** from less well-known parts of the organization, balance participation so that it doesn't favor either the most fluent or the most strident, and introduce simple, reliable frameworks for explaining differences and helping leaders to understand **"the why behind the behavior."** Such programs can also enable people to move beyond readily visible differences to discover **unexpected similarities**—for instance, a common military background, children of identical ages, or previous experience in the same country—which foster trust in a way that is less feasible if differences are ignored or downplayed. **Action learning that focuses on identifying and resolving practical issues** also generates common ground for participants through shared trials and joint problem-solving. **Inviting organizational leaders to recount their own developmental journeys** lets others know that it is okay to struggle while facing severe trials, reassuring them that they are not alone.

Cultural Competence

The underlying framework for such learning is straightforward, moving from self-awareness to knowledge about others to techniques for building bridges in practical ways. This is in fact the core definition of "cultural competence," and it applies to crucible experiences both at home and abroad.

Figure 2.4 Cultural Competence: Three Steps[6]

1. Know yourself
2. Know others
3. Know how to bridge differences and build on similarities

Hannah de Zwaan from the Netherlands learned these lessons the hard way after moving to the Czech Republic and taking on a factory general manager role there.

> **Hannah the Factory Manager**
>
> *Hannah describes her original leadership style as "very much engaging in open, democratic*

discussion and involving staff in decisions." She soon discovered, however, that, "You need to be able to step outside yourself and get into the other person's head. Your way of doing things is just one of many... Where I came from, people want to be informed about everything, but when I was in the Czech Republic, at first I really over-informed employees and they were bored, sleeping through meetings. I was used to democratic management, but this did not work at all in the Czech Republic. The most difficult task was being responsible for eighty blue-collar workers who spoke no English. At first I had a warehouse manager, but he left and then I had no one, so I needed to deal with employees myself. I had to go out on the warehouse floor, take a box, show exactly how to pack it, and tell them to finish by 3:00 P.M. It felt like being in the army to be giving such specific directions. They immediately respected me and did what they were told to do. Because of the cultural differences I had to change my leadership style and become stricter, more directive, and provide clearer deadlines." As time went on, she also discovered that she had to differentiate between working with her production manager and with local blue-collar workers, becoming more or less directive in her leadership approach. "You have to be able to switch as needed to get results."

Many aspects of Hannah's leadership role were not easy, including her dealings with vendors outside the company. "I was the first woman general manager. I had to deal with the manager of a local company who was not cooperating. He saw me as a naïve female, and tried to slow things down and give me an unfair price. You have to be tough and not just accept people trying to fool or cheat you." She also struggled with the Czech language. "I ended up speaking a mixture of Czech and English to communicate. I tried to learn Czech, but it is a very difficult language. So I learned what I could and used it, and they respected me for this."

Hannah eventually found herself sharing her hard-won understanding of both sides of the cross-border interaction. "I had a lot of colleagues from headquarters come down to deliver training in the Czech Republic. They kept saying that Czech people are so different, but I would respond, "From their standpoint, you are very different. You are in their country so you are the one who is different."

Hannah developed great affection and respect for her local colleagues. "I learned a few lessons about Czech culture and history. This helped me to understand the reasons for why they are the way they are. The lack of initiative, for example, is linked to the communist period in their history. This is how you had to act to survive." As her own understanding and ability to adapt to local circumstances deepened, she found that a significant part of her job became managing others' expectations. "A lot of my time was used in setting the right expectations of people in other parts of the company, including headquarters. It is difficult for them to imagine what it is like, what is possible, what the price levels are, how the culture works. Being a bridge-builder and aligning expectations took a lot of time."

Crucible Learning: The Impact

Hannah's journey from self-awareness to understanding her colleagues to bridge-building not only made her a far more effective expatriate factory manager, but it also gave her hard-won leadership lessons that have stayed with her. She is now comfortable running a diverse multicultural team at headquarters. After moving back to the Netherlands, she was put in charge of a team that included six managers, all of different nationalities. Hannah notes, "I felt that it was so easy to get to know them, to start a dialogue and engage in small talk because I can easily imagine how they feel being here, what kind of problems they have being new to this country and not knowing the language. I can put myself in their place. I have more empathy." Her frame of reference, or perspective, as a leader has broadened, and she has become flexible enough to devise solutions for business problems by leveraging more than one perspective. "Sometimes I look at issues from the Czech point of view now."[7]

Other types of crucible experiences produce similar learnings, whether the distance between participants is defined by national borders or the gap between the assumptions and expectations of people from different backgrounds within the same country. For example, managers in the Czech Republic today, both expatriates and locals, note that they must respond to motivational differences between different generations if they are running a multi-generational team. These differences have been most strongly shaped by pre- and post-communist environments, depending on whether people were born before or after a communist-era baby boom that lasted until the early 1980s. Workers born in the communist period generally tend to be more risk-averse, hierarchical, and comfortable with structure, while younger workers who have grown up in a very different environment are more adventurous and entrepreneurial than the previous generation.[8] So a Prague-based project manager may need to ignore assumptions from elsewhere about the characteristics of "Gen X" or "Gen Y," as well as lessons acquired from handling the prior generation of workers, and learn how to build employee engagement and performance with multiple generations in local terms.

Those who go through crucible experiences of one kind or another report, like Hannah de Zwaan, that they must become clearer about their own background and assumptions, learn more about the people in front of them—including their individual personalities and predilections—and find ways to build ties of mutual understanding, trust, and practical action. Through the journey from self-awareness to other-awareness to bridge-builder, such experiences tend to foster several key capabilities that underlie inclusive leadership.

- **Empathy**: sensing the emotions of others, including reactions to exclusion

- **Perspective**: taking a broad and objective view of self and others

- **Flexibility**: altering behavioral patterns that are exclusionary and ineffective

Such critical leadership lessons are not easily spoon-fed or doled out as pre-packaged insights that can be weighed and measured, meanwhile shielding the learner from frontal exposure to real differences. They must be deeply learned and felt. Once absorbed, however, they often become enduring characteristics of successful leaders.

Addressing Unearned Disadvantages

Differences are generally most volatile when they intersect with access to power. For example, people who are members of minority racial or ethnic groups, non-native speakers of the organization's primary language, or female employees in a setting where women executives are few in number face many built-in disadvantages. While some leaders who are accustomed to being part of a dominant group may bristle at the notion that they are enjoying "unearned advantages," **many will appreciate and want to address the negative impact of "unearned disadvantages."** The fire of a crucible role is beneficial for any high-potential leader, and it can bring an especially keen appreciation for the consequences of exclusion and unearned disadvantages to those who have not previously known them first-hand.

All leaders can potentially learn from the profound and disorienting pain of separateness, of not belonging, of being a stranger who must build trusting relationships with new people in order to get things done. Those with access to institutional power and authority have a special responsibility to take the initiative and to lead by example. Bridge-building works best when it is practiced in concert with others, and employees closely watch those in positions of power and take their cues from them.

The empathy, perspective, and flexibility developed through crucible experiences foster a strong sense of kinship and future possibility across an organization. They are also indispensable ingredients for handling all forms of exclusion effectively, whether these are based in the past, present, or future. Perceptive leaders have a keen sense of an **expanded present** that contains both the legacy of many histories—"history is literally present in all that we do"[9]—and the potential for a better shared future.

CHAPTER THREE

Inclusive Behavior: Learning About Bias

Is there a concise approach to understanding and addressing unconscious bias?

Learning about Bias

Building Key Skills

Working Across Boundaries

Becoming a Champion

Getting Results

> Each of us has to extract ourselves from the box of assumptions that can keep us walled in and impervious to the ideas and capabilities of others.

Asim is a manager for a high-tech company who has been living in the U.S. for most of his adult life. He considers it his home—five years ago his employer sponsored him for a green card, which he cherishes. He is originally from India and is Muslim, although he does not practice all the tenets of the faith, such as praying five times a day.

> *I have lived in America for fifteen years, ever since coming for graduate school, but now for the first time I am afraid. I love America and it has given me and my family many opportunities. People were so welcoming when I first came to this country, and I made wonderful friends. Maybe it's just my perception, but at work now I feel that some colleagues are looking at me in a different way and worrying that I am a terrorist, although 9/11 was many years ago. I am afraid they look at my wife and children that way too. And it has become more difficult to travel back to India to visit my parents and return—in the airport now I am often 'randomly' selected for extra questioning, and on our last trip even my wife and children were held in a room and questioned. It was humiliating. Worse yet, we have heard recently about Sikhs from India who were heckled, beaten up, or had hot coffee thrown in their face right here in California, based on the mistaken assumption that they are Muslim. The people who are attacking them do not seem to realize that they are followers of a different religion.*

Inclusive Behavior #1: Learning About Bias

Now more than ever is a time to be a role-model for inclusive behaviors. Inclusive leadership is a process of bridge-building. It involves self-awareness, careful listening, outreach to people with different perspectives, and persistent, stubborn efforts to find common ground. It is founded on mutual respect—a consistent pattern of trustworthy behavior is also vital because trust is the currency of inclusion.

This is often easier inside an organization than across a whole nation, as employees of any organization ultimately share the common objectives of growing in key markets, becoming more efficient, and attracting and retaining competent and highly skilled talent. Successful corporate leaders build self-awareness of their own cultural backgrounds, invite unexpected information from employees and from new markets, and become catalysts for solutions that integrate diverse contributions.

National or organizational cultures, which embody shared knowledge and are themselves a collective means of survival, can also support forms of bias that are hard to detect...

Before any bridge-building can begin, however, **each of us has to extract ourselves from the box of assumptions that often keeps us walled-in and impervious to the ideas and capabilities of others.** "We can be blind to the obvious, and we are also blind to our blindness," notes the Nobel-Prize winning economist Daniel Kahneman.[1] Unconscious bias is a pervasive feature of the human brain, ultimately grounded in natural tendencies such as daily habits and instincts for self-preservation. More than half a century of psychological and anthropological research, now augmented by neuroscience and its access to functional magnetic resonance imaging (fMRI) data, has identified brain-based patterns of human behavior—"fight or flight," for instance—that are linked to survival and tend to reinforce bias. National or organizational cultures, which embody shared knowledge and are themselves a collective means of survival, can also support forms of bias that are hard to detect: "Culture hides much more than it reveals, and strangely enough what it hides, it hides most effectively from its own participants."[2]

Here are four types of unconscious bias, with examples of how they can inhibit productive interactions among employees of the same organization. Those who learn about such biases are likely to see them almost immediately in their own daily interactions, as they are powerful and mutually reinforcing elements of most people's lives.

Figure 3.1: Unconscious Bias: Four Types

Confirmation Bias

Insider Bias

Attribution Bias

Overconfidence Bias

1. Confirmation Bias

"We see the world as we are"—Anais Nin

Humans are creatures of habit, and much of our day is spent on autopilot, carrying out routine tasks. Our expectations are shaped by our previous life experience, and the automatic reactions we have as a result of these expectations—say, driving forward through a green traffic light with the assumption that other vehicles will remain stopped while their light is red—make it possible for us to get through each day in a way that is functional, efficient, and safe. However, even when our expectations are based on insufficient information and/or faulty assumptions, the same mental process still tends to run in the background, "confirming" that we have seen what we expected to see. This may include the expectation that individuals are friends or foes, competent or incompetent, suited or not suited for particular roles, or should be more or less closely managed because they are perceived as belonging to particular categories.

Because Asim is from South Asia and a Muslim, if he grows a beard, for example, other employees from different backgrounds may almost imperceptibly begin to feel that he has taken on radical beliefs because he now looks a bit more like those terrorists in the news. The real explanation may be that his wife thinks he looks better in a beard, that he finds it warmer to have facial hair during a rainy winter, or that he has taken on more responsibilities at work and is cultivating a new leadership image. Unless Asim's colleagues take the time to question their assumptions, they may find themselves avoiding him in the cafeteria or hesitating to endorse him when he is put up for promotion.

> *Recommendation:* One way for a leader to approach confirmation bias would be to reach out to Asim—inviting him to lunch instead of avoiding him—and learn more about him, asking about his interests, goals, and aspirations, just as a good manager might do with any other employee. In the process, it is important not to make Asim feel singled out for being "different," as this could make the situation worse instead of better. Learning more about Asim is likely to reshape assumptions about him based on more pertinent information, and thereby to recast daily perceptions of his actions. (Perhaps Asim is growing a beard because he lost a bet to his cousin that his favorite Bollywood star would get married this year.)

2. Insider Bias

"Beware of strangers."

For most of its history and prehistory, the human race lived in tribal units. Cities, countries, and corporations are relatively recent inventions. Our brains are wired to recognize and respond to threats to our survival, and to immediately recognize subtle cues regarding whether another person is part of what we regard as our "in-group," or a potentially hazardous "out-group."

Asim speaks English with a British accent, visits India over the holidays, and knows more about cricket than baseball. Even though he has lived in the U.S. for many years and is a legal resident, there are still aspects of his appearance that could seem "foreign" to some

U.S.-born workers who have not traveled widely. In a corporate context, inclusive leaders must actively counter the deep human instinct to distinguish insiders from outsiders.

> *Recommendation:* Widen the "in-group" circle by creating new markers of membership such as clothing with the company logo, team pictures, birthday celebrations, invitations to corporate events, honors and awards, and so on. It is difficult to be suspicious of a person who just received a nice award for his tenth anniversary with the organization.

3. Attribution Bias

"Sorry I'm late. The traffic was terrible."

More than sixty years of psychological research into "attribution theory" has provided insights into the ways in which humans explain behavior and events. When there is a problem, we tend to explain our own flaws in terms of circumstances, and attribute the mistakes of others to character defects; the reverse is true when the outcomes are positive. We attribute success to the positive character attributes of ourselves or close associates, while providing circumstantial explanations to rationalize the successes of others who are seen as outsiders.

Negative Outcome: If Asim is late for a team meeting, for instance, a counterpart might leap to the critical judgment, "He is not very well organized" (character), without noticing that Asim's previous meeting ran over because the business unit director wanted to address a customer issue on the spot (circumstance).

Positive Outcome: Conversely, when Asim's project team completes its project on time and under budget, this could be attributed to a terrific set of team members (circumstance), and not to his leadership style (character).

> *Recommendation:* Question character judgments, particularly regarding those who might not be perceived as insiders, by asking about mitigating circumstances. "Is he frequently late or was this an exception? Did he have a prior meeting?" Likewise, question whether attributions to circumstances (the team performed well because of its members) are obscuring real talents or demonstrations of character.

4. Overconfidence Bias

"All the children are above average."

Another enduring aspect of the human psyche is that we have greater subjective confidence in our judgments than an objective assessment would warrant. We also tend to overestimate our own performance relative to that of others. No one is exempt—generals, doctors, politicians, students, and corporate leaders all can fall victim to overconfidence. So in that nine-box succession planning meeting during which a colleague confidently asserts that "Asim is a high performer, but not a high-potential," it is important to ask for more evidence. Is this assertion based on the fact that Asim has a management style that is grounded in his cultural background? How has he responded to previous opportunities for professional development? Is he more suited to a technical track than a management track? How will you know?

> *Recommendation:* Test confident assertions, both your own and those of others, for signs that they are grounded in solid evidence. Systematically incorporate multiple perspectives and forms of evidence into processes such as succession planning to better ensure that assertions are examined from various points of view using balanced sources of data.

For those who find mnemonics useful, the Italian word **CIAO** has a dual meaning. It can signify greeting or departing, hello or good-bye. Each encounter that a leader has with fellow employees can be a greeting that is open to new information and possibilities, or a hasty act of avoidance due to faulty, unexamined assumptions. Remembering and running through the first letter of each of these forms of unconscious bias—**Confirmation, Insider, Attribution, and Overconfidence**—is one way of building greater awareness and ensuring that neither individuals nor their organizations fall victim to such bias. Once leaders can identify their own possible sources of bias, reexamine their perceptions, and seek fresh insight when needed, they are then able to make informed and flexible choices.

Empathy: The Doorway to Action

Addressing unconscious bias requires genuine effort. During the course of any given day, how can a leader with positive intentions but limited time cultivate a personal commitment to action?

Daniel Goleman's work on emotional intelligence highlighted the value of empathy for people in leadership roles.[3] Noting the neurological basis of psychological states such as fear and other forms of "emotional hijacking," Goleman attempted to explain why talented leaders sometimes fail, even though they may be technically gifted or have crafted a brilliant business strategy. Employees respond to their own managers in ways analogous to the manner in which patients evaluate physicians based on their "bedside manner." Physicians with equal medical acumen tend to either be evaluated positively by patients or sued more frequently for malpractice depending on how effectively they listen and respond to their patients' emotional states. Similarly, leaders who are able to perceive and respond to the emotions of others are more likely to build real trust, engage team members, and accomplish their overall objectives.

So what does empathy look like in a diverse workforce context? Most people will agree with the principle of equal opportunity for all, with advancement based on merit and performance. They are also usually willing to support others who have disadvantages stemming from factors difficult for them to control such as poverty, race, gender, educational opportunities, nationality, or other elements of an individual's life circumstances. Leaders who learn about the challenges faced by fellow employees like Asim are often inspired to take action—this is especially true when the workplace experiences and/or life histories of these employees become more vivid through a story or example that helps to arouse empathy.

Here is a sampling of the surprising range of comments made by employees who are struggling to succeed in a diverse workforce environment.

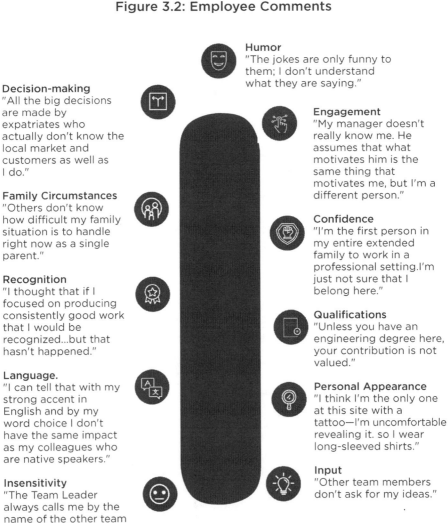

Figure 3.2: Employee Comments

Humor
"The jokes are only funny to them; I don't understand what they are saying."

Decision-making
"All the big decisions are made by expatriates who actually don't know the local market and customers as well as I do."

Engagement
"My manager doesn't really know me. He assumes that what motivates him is the same thing that motivates me, but I'm a different person."

Family Circumstances
"Others don't know how difficult my family situation is to handle right now as a single parent."

Confidence
"I'm the first person in my entire extended family to work in a professional setting. I'm just not sure that I belong here."

Recognition
"I thought that if I focused on producing consistently good work that I would be recognized...but that hasn't happened."

Qualifications
"Unless you have an engineering degree here, your contribution is not valued."

Language.
"I can tell that with my strong accent in English and by my word choice I don't have the same impact as my colleagues who are native speakers."

Personal Appearance
"I think I'm the only one at this site with a tattoo—I'm uncomfortable revealing it. so I wear long-sleeved shirts."

Input
"Other team members don't ask for my ideas."

Insensitivity
"The Team Leader always calls me by the name of the other team member from Mexico although we don't look alike."

Cultivating greater empathy toward workplace colleagues provides surprising dividends in return. For those who find it difficult to sit and contemplate how unconscious bias may be clouding their judgment or affecting their daily conduct, an advantage conferred by increased empathy is that it offers meaty possibilities for perceiving immediate and perhaps unintended responses to one's own actions. **Empathy not only dials us into the general emotional state of others, it allows us to see where we may have caused real damage ourselves.**

It could have been "me," for instance, who assumed that another person is motivated in the way that I am, who failed to reach out to a new employee, who internally scoffed at a tattoo, or who mistook one colleague for another with the same ethnic background. Maybe "I" forgot to ask others for their ideas (even though they were bursting to share them), felt impatient with a colleague's heavily accented speech, didn't offer recognition where it was due, ignored the challenges of a single parent, or made that insider joke that caused some people to feel left out. Leaders with a genuine desire to become more inclusive can learn quickly from their own mistakes through a positive feedback loop of empathy, insight, and reflection. Each reinforces the other, unlocking deeper empathic skill.

Figure 3.3: Empathy, Reflection, & Insight

Inclusive Actions

Our workplaces can promote either exclusion or inclusion. Nearly everyone has felt excluded at some point in their lives. Moving to a new school, being chosen last for a playground team, making the wrong wardrobe choice, encountering a physical or verbal bully, not hanging out with the popular kids, or doing poorly in math or art—these are all ways that people may feel like outsiders as they are growing up. Some are made to feel like perpetual outsiders based on aspects of their lives that they cannot change such as gender, age, skin color, etc. The stakes become far greater when exclusion is not only permanent, but also translates into tangible disadvantages in workplaces or communities, whether this means limited educational or employment opportunities, few chances for pay raises or promotions, or inadequate access to quality healthcare.

Inclusive leaders provide personal examples through their daily actions, setting the tone for their organizations and team dynamics. If we seek to harness the full energy, enthusiasm, and potential of each individual in a diverse workforce, it is vital to cultivate genuine empathy and find ways to better understand and include employees such as Asim along with others who have similar, but different life stories: Manuela, Marwan, Ayo, Sachiko, Leotie, Sergei, or Louise. Each name has a meaning, often unknown to co-workers, that only begins to point to the complexity of the person. It is essential for leaders and teams to be alert to the mental prison shaped by unconscious bias, and to recommit to the basic principles of listening, bridge-building, and creating common ground.

> **The stakes become far greater when exclusion is not only permanent, but also translates into tangible disadvantages in workplaces or communities...**

Learning About Bias: Summary

- **Demonstrate curiosity** when interacting with persons with different backgrounds and cognitive styles.

- **Check for bias in yourself and others**: Ask, "Are we relying on obsolete information or stereotypes?"

- **Flip it and test it:** Take your response to a situation and test it by checking to see if you would act in a similar way with a different person. If not, ask yourself if your immediate response was suitable.

- **Ask open-ended questions:** Encourage discussion and actively listen for new perspectives and experiences.

- **Check "Intent / Impact":** If what you said had a different impact on another person than intended, explore what you could have done differently.

- **Surprised by an answer?** If someone reacts in a way that you did not expect, ask what they are thinking and why.

- When discussing sensitive topics, **don't judge until you fully draw out the other person's point of view.** What information do you lack?

- **Request input!** Ask someone from a different background or culture about behavioral cues: what to expect, what is valued, etc.

- **Build empathy** by seeking to understand the experience of others who may have been excluded through no fault of their own.

CHAPTER FOUR

Unconscious Bias on a Global Team

 *What is the impact of increased inclusiveness on team performance?*

Unconscious bias is generally described and viewed through an individual lens. Learning programs focused on bias typically provide a list of potential biases, with explanations and examples of each, and ask participants to reflect on how **bias of one kind or another may be affecting their own conduct. However, bias acquires its most powerful forms in complex interactions—social, political, economic—in which an individual's views and behavior impact others and are impacted in return.** Social media is rife with biased commentary

> How can teams create a positive, upward-moving cycle of shared insight and high performance?

that can echo and grow, spark harsh clashes, or consist of people talking past each other; there is often little real dialogue between people who have different perspectives, and seldom any resolution. Another manifestation of such biased interactions, with vital implications for organizational performance, can take place within a global team.

Diverse global teams offer fertile ground for the propagation of bias due to a number of reasons:

- Remote team members may not have the chance to get to know each other well.

- Virtual communication and cultural differences in communication style make it easier for misunderstandings to occur and to fester.

- Team members are often dealing with "foreigners," or people far from their immediate in-group who look and talk differently.

All of these factors affect the development of a basic sense of trust as well as alignment among team members. It is not surprising that research on the performance of diverse teams shows mixed results. When they are inadequately managed, such teams tend to perform poorly, as differences and distance create strong centrifugal forces that pull them apart. On the other hand, teams perform at a higher level when they are managed in ways that enable their members to both "diverge," or draw out the creative potential of different perspectives, and "converge" by aligning around shared goals, clear roles, and a joint commitment to action.[1]

So how might bias affect a global team and what is the best way to address this? Self-awareness is a contact sport, and unconscious biases are most on display when people come into contact with others from different backgrounds. First, it is important to examine how the biases of team members can interact and result in mutual incomprehension and negative judgments.

Example: The Asia-Pacific Team Meeting

A meeting has just occurred in which the members of a product service team were brainstorming solutions to an urgent client issue in a series of rapid-fire exchanges. During the meeting, headquarters-based participants in London, including an experienced team member named Alex, did much of the talking, while the team members based in Singapore were mostly silent. Here are the post-meeting impressions of the team leader at headquarters, followed by a contrasting set of impressions from one of the Singapore team members:

> ### The View from Headquarters
>
> *I know that my colleagues in Singapore are less experienced. They usually don't have much to contribute to our meetings. I was disappointed but not surprised when they didn't say anything during our lively team discussion. I was impressed by the meeting contributions of my team member Alex, whom I've known for many years—we used to work in the same product group together when I was in a previous role. Alex had a lot to say during this meeting because he is an expert. Several of the other participants were too passive, and should have spoken up more. I felt that we had a good meeting overall, and identified solutions that would be effective throughout Asia-Pacific.*

> ### The View from Singapore
> *We knew that the team leader wasn't really interested in our opinions. He never gave us time to speak. People based at headquarters have a very limited understanding of our local clients and their*

> *needs. We could contribute more if they would study the data we send them in advance, and then would run meetings in a way that we can join in the discussion. Alex seems to like to hear his own opinion—he feels that he is the only expert, but he is just the one with the loudest voice. It is unlikely that solutions similar to those from other regions will work in Asia-Pacific.*

Analysis: Bias on a Global Team

Global team veterans are likely to recognize many of the challenges that this team is facing. Before leaping to best practices that this team could implement, it is useful to examine team member interactions for possible forms of unconscious bias, as this can be a source of insight for why they have become so unproductive. In Chapter 3 we outlined the **CIAO model of unconscious bias**, which is summarized here:

- **Confirmation Bias:** We see what we expect to see. With limited information, our brain fills in the blanks based on prior experiences and beliefs.

    Example: Both men and women tend to evaluate women candidates for technical roles more critically than they do male candidates.

- **Insider Bias:** Genetic programming for "signs of danger" divides us into allies (insiders) or enemies (outsiders or foreigners).

    Example: Managers tend to favor employees from the same university, region, or ethnic group as themselves.

- **Attribution Bias:** We "attribute" different causes to similar events based on whether someone is an insider (or ourselves) or an outsider. There are two opposite forms of attribution depending on whether the results are positive or negative: Insiders tend to be praised for positive results based on character, or excused for poor results due to circumstances. Outsiders are praised for positive results based on circumstances or, when things go badly, blamed for defects in character or aptitude (women, minorities, or foreign nationals are often subjected to this form of bias). In the following example, Edward is a close friend of the manager, and Gwyn is not.

Manager commenting on positive outcome: Edward's team is doing well because he is a strong team leader (character); Gwyn's team is performing well because she has a terrific set of team members (circumstance).

Manager commenting on negative outcome: Edward's team is struggling because he just doesn't have the right mix of team members (circumstance); Gwyn's team has problems because she is more tactical than strategic (character).

Confirmation Bias

Insider Bias

Attribution Bias

Overconfidence Bias

"CIAO" in Italian can mean either "Hello" or "Goodbye"!

- **Overconfidence Bias:** We are overconfident about our own judgment and about our competitive standing relative to others.

  Example: Over ninety percent of college professors believe that they are in the top half of teaching performers.[2]

Unfortunately for the members of the Asia-Pacific team described above, the CIAO model fits their interactions quite well. The comments of the two team members are revisited below with a breakdown that labels these four biases in action on both sides:

> ### The View from Headquarters
>
> **Confirmation Bias:** *I know that my colleagues in Singapore are less experienced. They usually don't have much to contribute to our meetings. I was disappointed but not surprised when they didn't say anything during our lively team discussion.*
>
> **Insider Bias:** *I was impressed by the meeting contributions of my team member Alex, whom I've known for many years—we used to work in the same product group together when I was in a previous role.*
>
> **Attribution Bias:** *Alex had a lot to say during this meeting because he is an expert. Several of the other participants were too passive, and should have spoken up more.*
>
> **Overconfidence Bias:** *I felt that we had a good meeting overall, and identified solutions that would be effective throughout Asia-Pacific.*

> ### The View from Singapore
>
> **Confirmation Bias:** *We knew that the team leader wasn't really interested in our opinions. He never gave us time to speak.*
>
> **Insider Bias:** *People based at headquarters have a very limited understanding of our local clients and their needs.*
>
> **Attribution Bias:** *We could contribute more if they would study the data we send in advance, and then would run meetings in a way that we can join in the discussion. Alex seems to like to hear his own opinion—he feels that he is the only expert, but he is just the one with the loudest voice.*
>
> **Overconfidence Bias:** *It is unlikely that solutions similar to those from other regions will work in Asia-Pacific.*

Team Member Bias: The Downward Spiral

The cumulative effect of such team member biases when they occur in combination is powerful and pernicious. First of all, the CIAO elements themselves are mutually reinforcing. Because some team members are perceived as relative outsiders (insider bias), it is likely that those who consider themselves insiders will expect and perceive negatives outcomes (confirmation bias), blame these outcomes on character flaws or lack of capability (attribution bias), and be convinced that their own judgment is correct (overconfidence bias). This lethal intermingling of biases is further compounded when there are negative views on both sides that reinforce the same patterns of unproductive behavior by confirming the biases that are fueling these behaviors in the first place. **A tail-chasing cycle of biased assumptions and actions makes everyone on the team less likely to seek out new information or to act in a way that would disconfirm their basic**

assumptions. Deeply entrenched views on both sides can make it harder to anticipate or to notice positive intentions or to elicit potential contributions, with slim prospect for change. Bias hardens into a wall of mutual blindness that causes teams to head into a downward spiral of misunderstanding, blame, misjudgment, and mistrust, all confirmed and deepened by poor performance.

Figure 4.1: Bias and the Downward Spiral

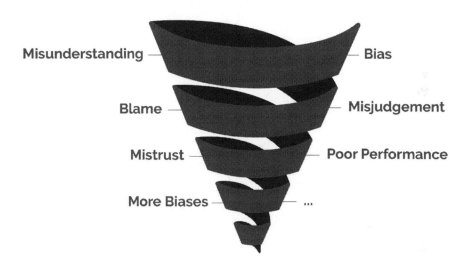

Global Teams: Best Practices

So how can teams avoid this frightening descent into mutual blindness and blame, creating instead a positive, upward-moving cycle of shared insight and high performance? Several decades of experience with global teams as well as empirical data suggest three specific areas of focus for countering bias and setting a team on a path for success: team foundations, cultural competence, and mutual learning.

1. Team Foundations

Among seven dimensions of global teamwork on a survey of over 1,300 teams and approximately 7,000 team members,[3] respondents consistently identify "Team Foundations" as the most critical dimension linked to high performance. In contrast with relatively homogeneous domestic teams, the members of which have a shared context of knowledge and practices, **teams with diverse global members need to regularly revisit these foundations** to counter the divisive effects of distance, differences, and even matrix organizational tensions. The foundations of global team performance include shared goals, clarity regarding roles and responsibilities, and adequate resources and cooperation from other parts of the company. In addition, one of the survey items most frequently selected across this large database refers to "a high level of trust among team members."[4]

Such empirical results overlap with recent research on the topic of "psychological safety"—one way to define this term is as a form of applied trust: "I trust that if I speak up, my voice will be welcomed and I will not be punished." A sense of trust or psychological safety may be a vital tonic for a diverse team because it counteracts several forms of bias simultaneously, supporting the creation of a new set of linked mental habits: we are more inclined to anticipate and "confirm" positive contributions by trusted members of our team, which widens the circle of "insiders" and discourages negative character "attributions" while supporting more positive interpretations of bet-

Figure 4.2: Google's Project Aristotle[7]

Abeer Dubey
Director, People Analytics, Google

- Objective: To identify what differentiates high performing teams from those that struggle.
- Analyzed 180 teams of tech and sales employees (over 200 interviews).
- Identified key features of successful teams, including **psychological safety**.
- "*Psychological safety allows teams to harness the power of diversity. That's because employees who have different points of view feel safe bringing their ideas to the table.*"

ter performance; "overconfidence" about faulty assumptions is also displaced by changing perceptions of team members.

Psychological Safety

Harvard researcher Amy Edmondson offers the following definition: "Psychological safety is a shared belief held by members of a team that the team is safe for interpersonal risk taking." She notes that this includes "a sense of confidence that the team will not embarrass, reject or punish someone for speaking up."[5] In diverse environments, which can easily devolve into sub-groups of insiders and outsiders, competing factions, or even opposing tribes in larger organizations, team members who perceive themselves or are perceived by others as relative "outsiders" are especially unlikely to speak out or to take risks. This phenomenon can be reversed as the sense of safety grows.

Google's Project Aristotle, which examined the factors correlated with success in a study of 180 internal teams, found that psychological safety was the single most important variable correlated with team effectiveness. Moreover, they discovered that although diversity alone was not a predictor of high team performance, **diverse teams *with* a high degree of psychological safety did perform at higher levels overall**. In other words, psychological safety is a vital ingredient of the "secret sauce" that enables diverse teams to realize their full potential.[6] Specific team characteristics associated with psychological safety include roughly equal air time for meeting participants and the readiness of team members to share incomplete ideas and their own personal vulnerabilities.

2. Cultural Competence

Team foundations must be built with an awareness of culture—otherwise team members may be unwittingly imposing their own preferred styles on others. Even the basic team building-block of trust is conveyed and interpreted in different ways, so the actions required to create a foundation of psychological safety are not the same everywhere. For instance, the statement, "Jump in any time with your questions and comments"—the expectation of the London-based team leader in the opening scenario—would be readily interpreted by colleagues from the same cultural background as an open invitation to contribute to a discussion. However, others from a different cultural environment may perceive this same invitation to be risky and insincere, or they may lack the skills to participate in such a manner. Elsewhere we have covered various factors perceived as signs of trustworthiness through different cultural lenses.[8] The chart below provides a list of sample trust-building actions by team leaders that are likely to be more or less effective depending on the cultural context:

Figure 4.3: Trust-Building: Cultural Comparisons

Trust-Building: Cultural Comparisons	
Independent *Tell me what you think.*	**Interdependent** *I'd like for you to meet as a small group and then share your thoughts.*
Egalitarianism *Don't worry about who else is in the room. The managers are just here to observe.*	**Status** *The boss has asked us all to come up with the best possible solution together, and expects us to have this by next Monday.*
Risk *Jump in any time with your questions and comments. We're all just brainstorming here, and any ideas are good.*	**Certainty** *I am sending you the agenda in advance so that you have time to prepare.*
Direct *I disagree with your last comment.*	**Indirect** *Please tell me more about your last comment.*
Task *We have a full day of work ahead of us, and then those of us who still have the energy can go out to dinner together.*	**Relationship** *We'll have dinner together the evening before our meeting so that those who haven't yet met in person can get to know each other.*

Cultural competence in a global team environment means moving beyond cultural awareness to apply the three-part formula outlined in Chapter 2: know yourself, know others, bridge differences. The team profile here portrays culturally-based work-style preferences of the global team members in London and Singapore.

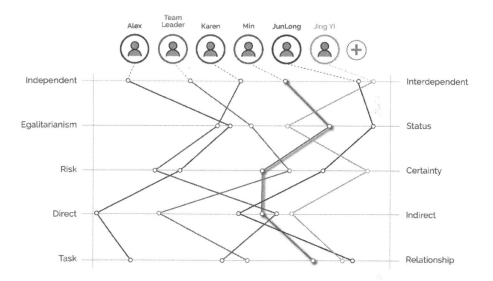

Figure 4.4: GlobeSmart Team Profile

The London-based team leader has a personal profile that is more "Independent," for example, than the profiles of other team members. Awareness of this contrast could prompt the leader to set aside a personal preference for more individualistic forms of expression—"Just speak up if you have something to say"—and modify the team meeting format to incorporate more group-oriented processes such as turn-taking, pausing the meeting to request comments in a virtual chat box, or allowing side discussions for small groups to solve problems. It may be necessary to take these steps on multiple occasions in order to set a new tone, to familiarize team members with the format, and to confirm the sincerity of the request.[9] At the same time, the team leader could strive to notice and learn more about the indirect signals that team members have been sending rather clearly in their own view.[10] This might require one-on-one conversations with a Singaporean team member to build a stronger relationship and to ask for guidance: "What could we do to get the other team members more involved? They've been pretty quiet during our meetings."

The bridge-building formula through which cultural competence is applied also counteracts each of the forms of unconscious bias outlined previously: "overconfidence" is supplanted by active inquiry, "confirmation" of mutually-held negative expectations is challenged with a new process that encourages wider contributions, and "attribution" is replaced with more real-time profiles that reflect the culturally-based tendencies of team members, helping to explain the "why behind the behavior." Most importantly, previous factional lines on the team that favored headquarters-based "Insiders" are at least partially dissolved, as all team members are invited to become active meeting participants. These actions will make the outward manifestations of psychological safety, including roughly equal airtime among team members and readiness to share ideas, far more likely to flourish.

3. *Mutual Learning*

Another characteristic of high-performing teams, according to Google's Project Aristotle, is constant mutual learning among team members. A team foundation of trust and psychological safety, bolstered by culturally competent bridge-building, surmounts the barriers of unconscious bias and provides the launch point for a positive cycle of shared discovery and learning. For example, The director of Google X, Astro Teller, has helped teams achieve superior results by holding "*pre*-mortem" sessions during which team members are asked to highlight possible reasons that a team project could fail.[11] By seeking out flaws in new ventures, in spite of the possible hazards associated with criticizing executive pet projects or simply being wrong about anticipated problems, Teller's teams are able to address potential failure points at an early stage. Team members clearly need to feel free to take risks, to speak up, to admit personal failings, and to learn from each other in such an environment.

Successful global team leaders instill the team discipline, "invite the unexpected," and link this with "frame-shifting" in terms of communication, leadership style, and strategic thinking.[12] In contrast to the negative cycle displayed earlier, in this case there is a positive spiral of trust, applied cultural competence, mutual learning, and high performance, with each of these steps further disconfirming lingering forms of bias and replacing them with realistic aspirations and heightened trust.

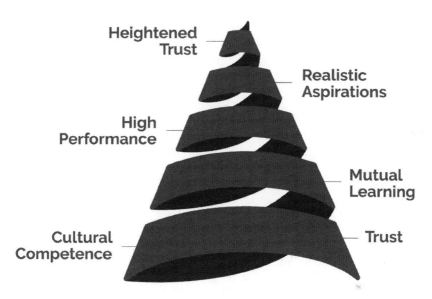

Figure 4.5: The Upward Spiral: Bias Unraveled

Those who have been in a strong mutual learning environment on a diverse team report that this is an unforgettable personal and professional experience. The team is "on fire" (in a good way) with ideas, energy, and creativity. Team members receive positive feedback not only from each other but also from internal and external customers, and the results that they achieve can turn them into the corporate version of rock stars. A more significant, intrinsically motivating side to this high-performing team equation, however, is the almost daily insights that team members gain in their work together, and the inspirational way that these insights are shaped into innovative products, services, and processes. Here are some comments from members of such teams:

At first we actively disliked each other and there was very little trust, but after we realized that we were serving different stakeholders and were able to better align our goals, we actually began to develop real friendships and to get things done.

We accomplished more in the past two days meeting together face-to-face than in the entire previous six months because now we know each other better and have a real foundation of trust.

At some point people stopped advocating for their own preconceived ideas and started listening to each other. That's when we really got creative.

I can't even remember where this idea came from— it seems like we all contributed.

Sometimes we end up with a completely different solution than what I was expecting because I listen to all players.

If I see that people have been marginalized in a situation, I will specifically bring them into the circle, inviting them to participate in making decisions whenever they can contribute.
The client insight came from our local salesperson, who knows the client better than anyone. The technical solution came from a client visit he made together with one of our corporate R&D experts— the conversation they had with the client led to a whole new package of products and services that our team has now rolled out to other markets.

My headquarters-based team member helped me to find the contact person I was looking for. She told me in five minutes what it would have taken me five hours to find on my own.

> *I had no idea about the realities of that market—the regulatory hurdles, the competition, the challenges in finding and keeping good talent. Thanks to our local colleagues we now have a much better go-to-market strategy.*

Global Teams: Retaining a Performance Edge

A high-performing team needs to stay on its toes, and mutual learning should be a constant discipline. Ironically, as team members get to know each other and become more aligned, they must be on guard against a stealthily accumulating "group-think" of the kind that commonly produces blind spots for more homogeneous teams. Increased mutual comfort among an expanded group of "insiders" may lead to the formation of habits that contain resurgent biases against yet another group of perceived "outsiders": new team members, related project teams, or different functions.[13]

In other words, **for the team to retain its positive momentum and to avoid slipping back into destructive habits, the mutual learning must continue**. Team members will need to keep expanding their circle of inquiry and insight by questioning established processes and incorporating fresh ideas and sources of information. The practice of "continuous learning" was taught long ago by the quality guru William Edwards Deming, and some of its underlying principles have applications far beyond factory floors if they are coupled with real inclusiveness in diverse team settings. There are a number of global team best team practices that are particularly conducive to ongoing mutual learning. Here is a summary list:

Mutual Learning: Global Team Best Practices

- **In-Person Meeting**: Preface the team's work by meeting face-to-face to pay special attention to team foundations (trust; stakeholder analysis; shared goals; roles and responsibilities) while building relationships in person.

- **First-Hand Observation**: At least the team leader and ideally all team members should visit each other's work sites to increase shared understanding through joint meetings and conversations with local stakeholders and customers.

- **Window Persons**: Exchange individual team members on a long-term or short-term basis so that there is a person in each key location who knows the people and the issues faced at other sites.

- **Tag Teams**: Establish "tag teams," or pairs of individuals based in different locations (e.g., headquarters and subsidiary) who work well together and can integrate contrasting perspectives.

- **Check-ins**: Plan for one-on-one check-ins with key team counterparts before and after meetings to ensure that agendas include key issues and vital information is exchanged.

- **Meeting Process**: Set up a regular meeting process with clear expectations for when and how team members will be expected to contribute; provide opportunities to prepare in advance.

- **Show and Tell**: Dedicate a portion of the team's meeting time to have team members describe unique aspects of their markets that the rest of the team might not know about.

- **Virtual Communication**: Use video cameras and combine voice communication with instant message exchanges to increase opportunities for team members to send and receive ideas; add texting and chat functions outside of meetings to supplement email with other channels.

- **Information Sources**: Incorporate additional types of information into the team's review process that reflect unfamiliar market realities, sources of competition, or emerging opportunities.

- **Catalyst Role**: The team leader or meeting facilitator takes the role of "catalyst," seeking to identify and integrate good ideas regardless of their source, building joint solutions rather than being an advocate for a particular point of view.

- **Risk-Taking**: Recognize or reward team members willing to take measured risks to reinforce the value of learning from both success and failure.

- **Expand the Circle**: Invite members of other groups to join the team's discussions where relevant to expand team member awareness, broaden networks, and contribute different perspectives and ideas.

- **"Winner" Identity**: Take note of and celebrate team successes—even initial quick wins—that stem from mutual learning in order to underline the value of such learning and to build the readiness of team members to take part.

CHAPTER FIVE

Inclusive Behaviors: Building Key Skills & Working Across Boundaries

What practical steps can leaders and employees take to become more inclusive?

Learning about Bias

Building Key Skills

Working Across Boundaries

Becoming a Champion

Getting Results

> An accumulation of micro-inequities creates a workplace environment that feels benign or even friendly to some but pervasively hostile to others.

Awareness of unconscious bias, including its effect on one-on-one interactions and within a global team, can either become a perpetual mental quicksand or a platform for action. How can people move from awareness to action? This chapter examines two further stages in the inclusion journey. Although each stage does build on prior ones, the journey described here is not necessarily linear. Leaders who focus on taking relatively simple inclusive steps may find that these become a catalyst for deeper insight into their own unintended biases; such insight can then enable more thoroughgoing action and behavior change.

Inclusive Behavior #2: Building Key Skills

The most critical inclusion challenges for those in management or supervisorial roles tend to occur with common tasks such as employee engagement, feedback, and meetings. Focused efforts on skill-building to address each of these topics are likely to produce practical results. Leaders who learn about their colleagues and develop empathy toward those who are experiencing some form of exclusion become better equipped to act in a targeted and effective manner. Perhaps the best way to illustrate how to respond to such employee concerns is to consider specific examples.

Example: Carla

Carla is a relatively new employee in her current workplace. Her parents had an elementary school education, and she is the first person in her entire extended family to be working in a professional white collar setting. Carla's biggest current issues are confidence and a sense of belonging—even after a year of employment at her new company, she still doesn't have the sense that she quite belongs, and often feels left out of discussions that involve humor she doesn't understand, unfamiliar acronyms, or banter among long-time team members.

> *Carla has reached out to make friends and has tried to learn quickly about her role and about her new work environment, but has been hesitant to assert herself with more senior colleagues because she is worried that she might be perceived as being overly aggressive. Some days are better than others, but today was a particularly difficult one because Carla realized during a team meeting that she had been unaware of a serious technical issue that everyone else on the team knew about and had been discussing already.*

There are many possible avenues for Carla's co-workers to act more inclusively in this situation, including her direct supervisor and peers at the same level. Beyond organization-wide programs for new employee onboarding, **there is typically an extended period required for new employees to get up to speed in their roles and to feel like they truly belong, particularly if they have entered a work environment that seems "foreign" based on their prior experience.** Actions that any peer can take based on a modicum of self-awareness and a sense of what could be helpful to a new colleague include simply reaching out and introducing oneself, initiating a conversation at the water cooler or coffee station, inviting Carla to join a group lunch,

"When I look around the office, I don't see a lot of persons like me – I don't feel that I belong here..."

"Yesterday was my best day so far. A few colleagues asked me to join them for lunch."

or offering to help her with an unfamiliar task. Each of us has a daily routine along with tasks to complete, and it may require a conscious effort to alter this routine slightly to include a new person.

Carla's supervisor should take additional steps to ensure that that she is effectively integrated into the team and able to fulfill her new role:

Figure 5.1: Integrating New Team Members

- Learn more about the new employee as a person to find out about professional aspirations, perceived strengths, and key motivators, along with possible concerns.

- Position this employee with other team members by sharing aspects of her prior background and experience (enough to make other team members feel welcoming yet not resentful of a new "golden child").

- Create a learning path with the new employee to build a sense of confidence and direction.

- Ensure that initial milestones are clear and reasonable, and check in frequently during the startup period to confirm understanding and progress.

- Translate acronyms, technical jargon, and insider humor to facilitate a sense of belonging.

- Provide feedback in an even-handed way to ensure that she knows how she can continue to make performance improvements.

- Extend invitations to team social events, and act as a role model for including this person in conversations on such occasions.

- Ensure that the new person gains access to information that longer-term employees are receiving through informal channels.

Example: Maksims

Maksims is an engineer, originally from Latvia, who is currently working in his company's European headquarters in Belgium. He was brought in as a mid-career hire, and is now concerned that the move he made with such optimism may turn out to be career-limiting. Maksims has a relatively introverted personality, and is a careful thinker who is slow to speak out not only by nature but also by choice—his motto is to think three times before saying something in order to ensure that his comments are both correct and considerate of others. His own Latvian cultural background has reinforced this, with long pauses in conversations being common among his family members and others from his home country.

Maksims was always better at engineering than at English during his university career. Although his foreign language skills are adequate, he finds that it is very difficult to contribute to team meetings that include forceful contributors as well as native English speakers who seem to enjoy debating and expressing their opinions vigorously. Maksims finds it distressing to listen to technical discussions that are apparently based on insufficient data or shaky assumptions, and he is a gifted engineer with an incisive critical mind and creative ideas to offer. However, he has not yet found a way to make a useful contribution to these meetings.

Nearly every company has the problem of one-sided meetings, with a few people doing most of the talking. A simple goal for leaders who seek to create more inclusive teams is to **make every conversation multi-directional, with anyone present who could make a useful contribution able to join the discussion**. Facilitating an inclusive team meeting is a skill that includes monitoring the conversation for contribution levels, noticing who could still provide useful input but has not, and asking more active participants to make way for others while drawing out the views of those who have been slower to speak up.

"People who are promoted here have an aggressive style and verbal skills in English that I lack."

"My team members know that I get results and have supported me for the new project leader role."

Given that their team includes non-native language speakers and divergent communication styles based on cultural and/or personality differences, Maksims' colleagues clearly need to implement a comprehensive set of best practices for team meetings if they want to leverage the full value of his engineering expertise (see also the list of recommended teamwork practices in Chapter 4). Their current team meetings feature lively exchanges among aggressive communicators who are fluent in English, but which discourage contributions from Maksims and probably others who are less than fluent and/or prefer to communicate in different ways. The following graphic provides suggestions for what the members of this team can do before, during, and after team meetings in order to ensure that their meetings are inclusive. It includes multiple means of ensuring that team members who are normally reticent have ample opportunities to speak.

Figure 5.2: Effective Team Meetings

Before
- Request input on agenda
- Send information ahead of time to enable preparation
- Communicate expectations for what should be prepared
- Time Zones: "Share the Pain"
- Specify desired outcomes
- Share information about attendees

During
- Identify a point person in each location to help facilitate the meeting
- Introduce speakers; allow time for informal relationship-building
- Structure breaks for local language discussions
- Provide extra time for those not verbally active
- Use instant messaging to support spoken language ability
- Use turn-taking or assigned roles for balanced participation
- Take live notes and summarize key points

After
- Send minutes and actions; request feedback
- Follow up informally with key individuals
- Determine if appropriate to cc others not present

Barriers to Inclusion: Micro-inequities

Another general skill-building area for anyone who seeks to act inclusively is to become aware of so-called "micro-inequities" that undermine positive intentions. Many otherwise talented workplace leaders find it easy to overlook or underestimate the impact of small behaviors of their own that may be perceived by others as exclusionary. Micro-inequities, in contrast with the "isms" (racism; sexism) that are more readily identified and linked with specific language or behaviors, tend to be relatively subtle and subject to different interpretations.

The list of possible micro-inequities overlaps with behaviors that in other contexts might be regarded as simply rude or inconsiderate. Contextual factors that differentiate micro-inequities from everyday boorishness and poor manners include conduct on the part of people in positions of authority that limits input from those who are seen as as outsiders, foreigners, subordinates, or juniors. Seemingly minor actions may be perceived as loaded with symbolism, and also taken as cues by other employees who begin to mimic this conduct. **An accumulation of micro-inequities creates a workplace environment**

Figure 5.3: Micro-inequities vs. Macro-inequities

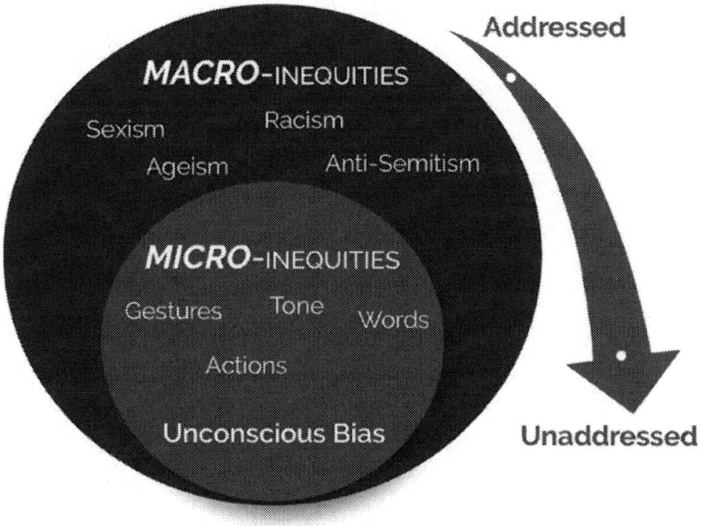

MACRO-INEQUITIES: Sexism, Racism, Ageism, Anti-Semitism — Addressed

MICRO-INEQUITIES: Gestures, Tone, Words, Actions, Unconscious Bias — Unaddressed

Small behaviors, often unconscious = **MACRO** Impact

that feels benign or even friendly to some but pervasively hostile to others. The good news for leaders who aspire to be more inclusive is that many of these behaviors, once noticed, are fairly easy to reverse or correct, and such positive symbolism is usually quite meaningful as well. Here is a list of sample micro-inequities and the unintended exclusionary messages they may convey, along with suggestions for how to address them.

Figure 5.4: Sample Micro-inequities and Possible Antidotes

Checking a smart phone during an important conversation

- **Perceived message:** *The person whose text the manager is reading is more important than I am.*

- **Possible antidote:** Put the phone down and turn off the sound, or at least apologize if you have to take a call or respond to a text: "Sorry, this is a text from my son whom I've been worried about. Would you mind if I send him a quick response?"

Greeting one person more warmly than others

- **Perceived message:** *My manager has a favorite employee, and it's not me.*

- **Possible antidote:** Greet each person in the room or in the workplace in a similar way, except in unusual cases such when a person has returned from a long trip.

Introducing one person with glowing accolades, and another with only a name

- **Perceived message:** *My manager values that person more than me.*

- **Possible antidote:** Make a conscious effort to introduce people in a similar way.

Omitting someone from an important e-mail or other form of communication

- **Perceived message:** *They don't feel the need to include me.*

- **Possible antidote:** Make a habit of taking one more step before you hit the send button to ask yourself who else should be included as a team member with something to contribute. (It's also important not to overdo this and copy others unnecessarily.)

Excluding an employee from socializing opportunities

- **Perceived message:** *I'm not part of the inner circle of this team.*

- **Possible antidote:** Consider whether there are others who would appreciate an invitation from fellow team members.

Taking credit for someone else's work or idea

- **Perceived message:** *Even when I have a good idea I'm not going to be recognized for it.*
- **Possible antidote:** Offer credit where it is due. (This will make you look like a better leader anyway.)

Cutting off a colleague in mid-sentence

- **Perceived message:** *They are not interested in what I have to say.*
- **Possible antidote:** Let the person finish, even if their communication style or language skills are different from yours.

Repeatedly canceling meetings with a colleague

- **Perceived message:** *Meeting with me is not a priority.*
- **Possible antidote:** Ask yourself why, apologize, and schedule a meeting for which you are fully present.

Using acronyms that others do not understand

- **Perceived message:** *They have a special language for insiders here and I don't understand what they're talking about.*
- **Possible antidote:** Explain the acronym you're using just like radio hosts explain unfamiliar terms used by guest speakers; if there are numerous acronyms that are difficult for new people, then create a list.

Exhibiting impatience because of a colleague's accent

- **Perceived message:** *I have a permanent disadvantage in this organization, no matter how good my ideas are.*
- **Possible antidote:** Try learning a foreign language yourself for a dose of humility and consideration. Practice speech without slang, idioms, or acronyms while modifying your pace of speaking; check periodically for questions and confirmation of understanding.

Only considering people with styles similar to yours for leadership and growth opportunities

- **Perceived message:** *The selection process for leaders here favors a certain type of person, and that's not me.*
- **Possible antidote:** Ask yourself if the only high-potential individuals are those you recognize in the mirror.

Expecting others to accommodate your time zone

- **Perceived message:** *They assume that their schedule and family life are more important than ours, or they don't really want me to attend anyway.*
- **Possible antidote:** Share the pain; acknowledge and thank others when they do.

Inviting a person to attend a meeting or function based on appearance rather than on substance or potential contribution.

- **Perceived message:** *Looks like I'm the token minority at this event; they don't really want me to contribute.*
- **Possible antidote:** Ensure that an invitation to attend includes a meaningful role.

In addition to the general list of micro-inequities that almost anyone can engage in without negative intent, the most crucial micro-inequities for managers and supervisors tend to cluster in five key areas. Focused efforts on skill-building to address each of these topics are likely to produce the best results. As with other aspects of this topic, many of the effects are unintended, and deliberate attention accompanied with straightforward actions can produce quick improvements.

Figure 5.5: Managers and Supervisors: Common Micro-Inequities

Meetings: Unbalanced Meeting Participation
"The same people do all the talking."

Delegation: "Throwing Things Over the Wall"
"I don't have enough information, and I am getting responsibilities thrown at me without having the opportunity to agree/disagree!"

Feedback: Conversations that Do Not Occur
"It seems like my supervisor is avoiding me."

Decision-Making: Not Consulted
"Nobody asked me."

Employee Engagement: Key Motivators are Assumed
"My supervisor said, 'I think you'll be really excited about this project.'"

Some micro-inequities have large-scale career impacts. For example, a leader's well-meaning assumption about what is right for an employee in terms of personal motivation or family circumstances may convey the message that this person is no longer on the fast track to an executive role. Such a misunderstanding could potentially be avoided by scheduling a conversation to explore the topic together.

> ### A Soft Landing?
>
> *An executive group was considering the best candidates for a new project team leader position. This role would involve considerable travel to a variety of locations in Asia-Pacific. The two top candidates under discussion were Luis and Karin, who both had strong track records. Another candidate was discussed briefly: "What about Tina? She is just coming back from maternity leave, and has been a star performer." A senior leader responded, "You're right. She's very capable, but I think it would be too much to ask her to do all that travel. Better to put her in a job where she can have a soft landing and not jump into such a demanding role right away." The team returned to discussing Luis and Karin, ultimately deciding on Karin for the role. Afterwards, it turned out that Tina would have appreciated being considered seriously. "At least they could have asked me what I wanted rather than assuming that they knew. My husband's work is flexible, and we both have parents living nearby who are happy to help with childcare. It feels like I've just been shifted from the fast track to the slow track in this company."*

The examples provided thus far illustrate how practical actions taken on a daily basis can address forms of exclusion that might otherwise affect the performance of individuals, teams, and entire organizations. Below is a more comprehensive list of key skills for creating an inclusive workplace. Both leaders and individual contributors will be able to identify many actions that they can take. We recommend starting with one or two that feel most accessible, and generating momentum with these while building on a team foundation of psychological safety that rewards input from all team members, reasonable risk-taking, and mutual learning.

Building Key Skills: Summary

Relationship Building

- How well do you know the people around you? What could you do to get to know them better? Express a sincere interest in learning more about them, listen carefully to what they say, and set a comfortable tone of discussion to draw them out further.

Communication

- Commit to being an **active listener**, aware and mindful of potential differences in communication style.

- Monitor your role in **workplace conversations**; consider whether you contribute too much or too little.

- Consider whether your **non-verbal messages**—conveyed through tone, body language, gestures, mobile phone usage, etc.—are consistent with your intent and are mindful of differing norms and preferences.

Motivation

- Create opportunities to ask or to observe **what motivates others**. Reflect on the differences between key motivators for yourself and others, and how to best address what motivates the latter.

- How can you draw out untapped skills or interests of your colleagues so they feel more engaged at work?

Feedback

- When providing feedback to others, are you **even-handed** with everyone, regardless of their background?

- Does your feedback include **recognition and reinforcement** for those who are willing to take risks, admit failures, and point out possible flaws in the team's approach?

- **Consider how often you seek feedback** on your actions from a peer, mentor, or "cultural guide."

Teamwork

- Actively consider **diverse competencies and profiles** when building teams.

- Provide meeting **agendas and materials in advance** so that non-native language speakers have time to prepare.

- **Structure meetings** with devices such as turn-taking, opportunities for written input, etc. so that each team member with something to contribute can join the conversation.

- Ensure that those who **take risks** by offering ideas or admitting mistakes are recognized and not punished.

Inclusive Behavior #3: Working Across Boundaries

While having an awareness of unconscious bias and a baseline set of inclusion skills in place often produces visible positive results, there is sometimes a tendency to declare victory too early. Heightened awareness and building key skills can lay the groundwork for further inclusive actions. Even for organizations that have achieved important statistical milestones—for example, increased retention of minority employees, or target percentages of women in managerial roles—there are far more ways to be inclusive.

People who have begun to build capabilities for working with colleagues from different backgrounds often encounter fresh opportunities to work with a wider range of counterparts representing additional diversity factors such as race, gender, age, nationality, function, cognitive style, and so on. Skills acquired for working with one set of colleagues may transfer easily to other types of relationships, or they may need to be modified. Diversity experts like to portray a "diversity wheel" with concentric circles that fan outward from characteristics that are inherited to those that are acquired over a lifetime. One such version, adapted from the work of Gardenswartz and Rowe,[1] is depicted in Figure 5.6:

Figure 5.6: The Diversity Wheel

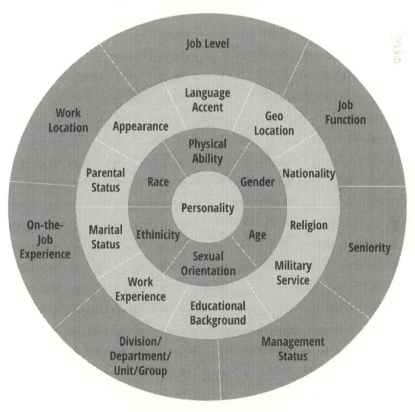

For those who seek to become truly inclusive, it is worth examining the current scope of their everyday business relationships, and asking where it would be useful to try crossing a visible or invisible boundary that separates them from other groups. To become sustainable, this should not be just a "nice-to-have" type of activity, but rather one that is based on business value. For instance, are potentially useful cognitive styles or technical skills that happen to be outside of the organizational mainstream valued and incorporated? (This could mean "blue sky" thinkers in a data-driven culture, or research and development scientists in a company built on marketing strength.) Are there individual personality differences, socio-economic gaps, or racial and ethnic distinctions that cause employees to feel excluded in a way that affects their level of engagement? Some boundaries, particularly those related to deep-rooted historical differences in access to power and resources, are more emotionally loaded and difficult to traverse. Others, such as organizational boundaries between functional roles, have been aspects of the human experience for millennia,[2] but are shifting as technology changes. Here is an example of a company that has encountered obstacles based on functional and geographical differences:

Superstars Versus Everyone Else

At a U.S. west coast-based information technology firm, employees complained about the bias that existed between technical employees in computer science or engineering functions and non-technical functions such as sales, finance, marketing, or human resources. Non-technical employees felt that they were being treated as second-class citizens. They wanted strategies for how to overcome this, yet the sources of bias were deeply ingrained.

The company had grown quickly through a series of hit product innovations. As it expanded throughout the world, the company's leaders recognized that their global presence had brought them a diversity of thought that could be a huge advantage in continuing their tradition of innovation and high performance. Many technical employees, even at headquarters, were originally from other countries, adding a further dimension of rich complexity. These were smart, ambitious, and forward-thinking people, so what was getting in the way of their truly being able to leverage the ideas and creativity of their entire workforce? The problem seemed to be behavioral habits that were grounded in the company's own original DNA and reinforced by its successes over time.

Employee interviews uncovered a culture in the organization that was open only to the ideas of those technical "superstars" who had been successful previously in product development, and who were primarily based in the United States. Most participants in the system considered themselves to be open-minded and without any particular bias—but there was a pervasive yet largely unconscious bias against those who weren't among the acknowledged superstars. Proposals from employees outside of the company's technical elite were viewed with skepticism, regardless of their value. In principle, people agreed that "we want an environment where all ideas are considered," but in reality, this was not happening.

Fifty employees came together in a room, and those who identified themselves as technical employees were asked for adjectives they would use to describe nontechnical colleagues. They used words like illogical, fuzzy, uniformed, uneducated, ignorant, and useless. Similarly, non-technical employees described their technical peers with terms like socially inept, passive-aggressive, self-absorbed, arrogant, territorial, and black-and-white thinkers. The starkly negative perceptions each group held of the other highlighted the importance of better integrating this functional dimension of diversity within the organization. Functional differences were clearly linked with an unhealthy dynamic that was impeding collaboration among different parts of the company. Surfacing negative stereotypes sparked intense and constructive

> *discussion about how to improve collaboration and generate ideas based on different perspectives to foster more deliberate cross-functional innovation.*[3]

In this example the barriers to innovation and higher levels of performance were primarily functional (tech vs. non-tech) but also cultural (home country vs. everywhere else). These barriers were further reinforced by widely held negative stereotypes that deepened divisions among conflicting factions and made attempts at collaboration seem pointless; loaded terms such as "illogical" or "arrogant" added fuel to the flames of mutual antipathy. To turn this situation around, employees in all parts of the world, including top executives, had to adopt boundary-crossing skills for approaching their counterparts with a new openness to mutual learning. The successful change effort that took shape over time incorporated a fresh organizational narrative—"We need each other to grow"—with an emphasis on positive examples of collaboration between technical and non-technical employees as well as those from different cultural backgrounds.

Global Boundaries

While organizational boundaries can be found wherever there are differences of any kind (race, gender, function), the most literal boundary lines are of course those drawn between countries. Do global colleagues who are remote from headquarters have an equal chance to advance based on their performance? Are they included in product development discussions that will affect their markets and their customers? Are they able to fully contribute their knowledge and capabilities to global team projects?

Physical distance, time zones, language barriers, and the limitations of virtual means of communication all reinforce national boundaries. In addition, culturally-based differences in leadership, communication, and problem-solving styles create even more significant gaps that global team members frequently underestimate or ignore. The five dimensions of culture depicted in Chapter 4 are based on many years of research and a very large database of survey responses. Knowing how one's personal cultural profile compares with those of global counterparts, customers, or team members is an excellent way to identify and bridge workstyle barriers, especially when the process takes into account the profiles of real people rather than inflexible stereotypes. In an increasingly mobile world with large waves of immigrants and refugees, it is more important to consider cultural differences within diverse local workplaces as well.

Global organizations offer yet another challenge for well-intended inclusion initiatives, as each country has its own unique constellation of diversity factors and priorities rooted in history and demographics. In a separate book, *Global Diversity*,[4] we have compared the diversity profiles of eight different countries, highlighting the factors that are most prominent in each location. In the absence of country-specific knowledge it is easy to make false assumptions such as, "Gender issues are the same everywhere," and to impose solutions from one's own social context onto another location where such measures may appear to be irrelevant or wrong-headed. Companies based in Europe, for instance, tend to highlight their own version of gender issues as well as employment challenges associated with ageism, while in Australia it is more common for organizations to wrestle with how to promote inclusion of indigenous people and large numbers of immigrants. A leader who seeks to become more inclusive on a global basis will find it worthwhile to consider the current social challenges and aspirations of employees in each major market. The table below outlines four country examples.

Figure 5.7: Contrasting National Diversity Profiles

United States	India
• Race and ethnicity • Gender • Religion and values • Regional origin and immigration • Sexual orientation	• Socioeconomic status • Regional origin • Religion • Gender • Language
Japan	**United Kingdom**
• Age • Gender • Regional background • Organizational affiliation	• Ethnicity and race • Regional origin • Socioeconomic status • Educational background • Language and communication

Personal Boundary-Mapping

A way to begin to identify where our own boundaries are drawn is by mapping our "go-to people" in the workplace. This exercise involves considering the people that we interact with most regularly in getting things done, analyzing how diverse this network is based on a number of factors, and considering whether business objectives could be achieved more readily by including people from different backgrounds. This exercise is described in Figure 5.8:

Figure 5.8: Go-To People Exercise

INSTRUCTIONS:

1. Write your name in the middle of the Mapping Activity page.
2. Around your name, write the names of key people at your company who are your "go to" people for input, strategic advice, delivery of critical projects, and thought partners. Note those who are in your most tightly held circle at your organization.

Individually:

Using different color markers, analyze the diversity dimensions of your "go to" people and draw connection lines as follows:

- **Black** - Different division
- **Green** - Different race or ethnicity
- **Red** - Different job level (at least 2 levels +/-)
- **Blue** - Different nationality and/or geographic region
- **Yellow** - Different age (at least 10 yrs +/-)
- **Purple** - Different gender
- **Orange** - Different regional and/or linguistic background

Leaders who seek to expand their "go-to network" based on this activity can ask themselves several questions:

1. How could you reach out to meet people from different backgrounds?
2. What could you do to learn more about them and see things through their eyes?
3. How might you adapt your own style to be more effective in engaging with them?

At the same time as we attempt to reach across boundaries to broaden our network and perspectives, it is vital to get to know real people rather than stereotypical categories, even revisiting labels that may appear to be familiar.

The "White Male" Category

Those who celebrate diversity sometimes ironically perpetuate a stereotype of white males. Whether the context is North America, Europe, Latin America, or the Middle East, a modicum of reflection reveals that this category incorporates a very heterogeneous mix.

People identified as white males may include, for example, individuals from radically different cultures and even bitter historical enemies: French, Germans, English, Scots, Croats, Serbians, Greeks, Turks, Italians, Spaniards, Algerians, Saudis, Israelis, Russians, Argentinians, and so on. White males are adherents of every major religion: Christianity, Judaism, Islam, Hinduism, Buddhism, etc. There are white males who are politically conservative and those who are radical, a mix of different sexual orientations, members of at least five different generations, native speakers of dozens of languages, city-dwellers and farmers, some who are well-educated and others who didn't finish high school, rich and poor, tall and short, factory workers and athletes, astronauts and homeless people. The traces of history still present within their everyday lives come from thousands of distinct social units, with memories, stories, poems, and songs echoing back to countless ancient campfires.

The fine lens of complexity that is so carefully applied by inclusion practitioners to other hot-button categories should be applied even-handedly to achieve a new and richer form of inclusiveness.

To further illustrate the practical steps involved in working across boundaries, it is worth examining another example.

Example: Lily

Lily works in her company's customer service call center in Chengdu, a city in southwestern China, where she is a newly promoted manager. She has now been placed on a project team that will require working with colleagues in the southern city of Shenzhen as well as a call center in the Philippines. Several of the Manila call center workers whom Lily will now be managing have been with the company for more than ten years and are significantly older than she is. Lily is open to this new management role but is feeling unprepared as she has no prior work experience outside of Chengdu. Some of her new Chinese colleagues in Shenzhen are native speakers of Cantonese, a different dialect that is difficult for her to understand, and she suspects that whatever perceptions she has about Filipinos are probably wrong.

In this scenario there are several types of boundaries that Lily will need to be able to cross in order to perform effectively in her new role: cultural, generational, and linguistic. Here are a few recommendations as she begins to manage her new team:

- Proactively build relationships with team members in other locations; learn about their backgrounds and the reasons behind their actions.

- Schedule initial "high-context" one-on-one meetings as well as team sessions that include video conference capabilities. Travel to Shenzhen and Manila to meet in person with the employees now reporting to her if this is at all possible budget-wise.

- Consider long-term or short-term rotations of team members between different locations to build greater shared understanding between sites and to have a "window person" to facilitate communication if necessary.

- Build a regular schedule that dedicates equal time to team members who are co-located and to those who are remote; reach out periodically to remote team members informally as well as formally.

- Learn everyday expressions in Cantonese, English, or Tagalog as a way to demonstrate interest and build ties with other team members.

- Handle long-term Filipino employees with respect based on their tenure with the organization, and ask for their advice on subjects in which they have special expertise.

- Refrain from making hasty judgments about team members based on insufficient information when problems arise, or when there is tension in a conversation.

- Find opportunities to give and receive feedback with colleagues in all locations.

For leaders who want to move beyond "Building Key Skills" and discover ways to apply their skills in an expansive workplace context, there are a number of pragmatic steps they can take. Organizational goals and personal job objectives are likely to drive boundary-crossing priorities. However, we often find that broad networks created based on genuine interest and friendships, without necessarily having an immediate task or goal in mind, can also offer significant personal and professional dividends over the long-term.

Working Across Boundaries: Summary

- **Examine your network**: Whom else can you reach out to in order to add more diversity to your network? Consider those from other functions, ethnic groups, generations, etc.

- **Create personal stretch goals**: Identify a group with which you are relatively unfamiliar (e.g., people from a different function) and learn more about those individuals. Monitor your biases and stereotypes (e.g., regarding the "millennial generation" or "Gen X"). Seek to discover different self-perceptions and/or patterns of behavior.

- **Pay attention to communication patterns** based on gender, generation, national culture, cognitive style, career experience, social class, etc.

- **Transfer skills**: If you have been successful in working with one group, try to transfer your skills to working with other kinds of people while being open to learning new skills as well.

- Consider **job switching, job shadowing, and job sharing** exchanges to broaden your experience.

- **Create an inclusive physical work environment**: Redesign your work space to be less "siloed."

- **Join diverse work teams** for exposure to different perspectives and to learn from each other in an inclusive team environment.

- **Seek input** (both formal and informal) to gauge the effect of current inclusion practices on groups that you do not know well; invite suggestions for improvement.

- **Organize and/or attend company-wide meetings**, celebrations, seminars, workshops, or retreats that bring together people from groups who do not normally come into contact with one another.

Figure 5.9: Personal Action Plan

PERSONAL ACTION PLAN

Select at least one of the following diversity dimensions, or another aspect of diversity you think is important in your place of work or study, and write down personal action steps you are willing to take in order to expand your own approach to inclusion.

- Generation
- Gender Identity
- Race/Ethnicity
- Culture
- Job Function
- CognitiveS tyle
- Disability

- Sexual Orientation
- Socioeconomic Status
- EducationalBackground
- Religious Belief
- PoliticalAffiliation
- Other

Keep the following questions in mind as you write down the action steps you will take below:

1. How could you reach out to meet people from the group(s) you have selected?
   _____
   _____
   _____

2. What are some things you could do to learn more about them and see things through their eyes?
   _____
   _____
   _____

3. How might you adapt your own style to be more effective engaging with them?
   _____
   _____
   _____

CHAPTER SIX

Inclusive Behaviors: Becoming a Champion & Getting Results

How can executives serve as champions and effective models of inclusion?

Learning about Bias

Building Key Skills

Working Across Boundaries

Becoming a Champion

Getting Results

> Getting results means not only blending the best ideas from different sources to create superior products or services, but also recruiting, retaining, and developing a diverse array of leaders who can drive future growth.

Many leaders have responsibilities that extend beyond the immediate business objectives of their own team. They must evaluate the performance and development potential of team members, contribute to cross-functional or interdepartmental meetings, interact with peers running other teams, deal with internal or external customers and suppliers, and manage upward to influence decisions made at higher levels in the organization. Beyond the inclusive behaviors covered previously—foundational skills for working inclusively with fellow team members and proactive extension of one's network to include a more diverse range of colleagues—there are ways that leaders can expand their organizational influence. Human resources departments may be in charge of providing a framework to manage and develop talent while enforcing compliance with legal standards; however, nearly everyone serving in a leadership role is involved in implementing multiple phases of the talent life cycle.

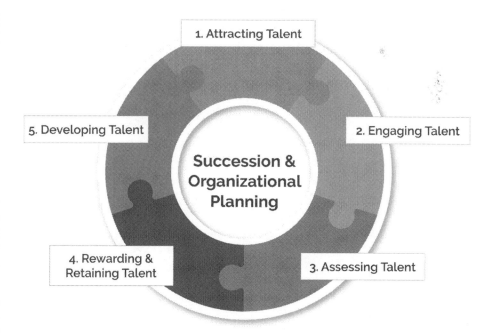

Figure 6.1: Talent Life Cycle

Inclusive Behavior #4: Becoming a Champion

Becoming a champion of inclusion involves recruiting diverse talent, building engagement among all employees, assessing performance and dispensing rewards fairly, retaining and rewarding high-potential individuals from any background, and developing future leaders—even people who don't fit current executive team member norms. Examining a couple of specific examples helps to illustrate how leaders can become champions of inclusion along the way.

Example: Katarzyna

Dr. Katarzyna Bankowski is a senior oncologist in a large hospital in Warsaw, Poland. In addition to her medical expertise, which is much admired by colleagues, she has a reputation for being an excellent listener who runs departmental meetings effectively. Her team consistently receives positive, even grateful feedback from patients as well. She did some of her previous medical training abroad, and therefore has experience with medical practices in several different countries.

Katarzyna has observed a retention problem at the hospital. Many young, newly qualified doctors who join the staff leave after their first year for medical residencies in the U.K., the Netherlands, Austria, and Germany. Based on conversations with departing physicians, she has learned that they often perceive the "old guard" of established physicians as being overly rigid and unwilling to adopt new patient care practices. Katarzyna wants to make the workplace more inclusive so that these young physicians feel they can build their careers in Poland rather than abroad.

Katarzyna's institution is experiencing the classic talent life cycle issue of how to retain high-potential employees, with a generation gap between older and younger physicians. If younger physicians continue to depart in large numbers without returning, the facility will suffer a talent drain that affects the workload of remaining physicians and ultimately the quality of patient care. Katarzyna could take steps such as the following to address the larger organization issue of excessive turnover:

- Understand more about the perspectives of the other senior physicians.

- Learn what motivates the younger doctors, including which changes they feel are most important.

- Recommend and model the creation of "reverse mentoring" pairs of senior and junior doctors who seek to learn from each other.

- Challenge the senior medical staff to improve the engagement and retention of younger physicians through a change initiative.

Each of these steps builds on prior stages of inclusive leadership. Katarzyna is already an effective, inclusive team leader with a diverse informal network of friends and contacts within the hospital. If she chooses to take these steps, she will have also moved beyond her own specific job description to tackle a broader organizational issue linked with the talent life cycle. Inviting senior and junior doctors to enter into mentoring roles with each other and challenging senior medical staff colleagues to improve the engagement and retention of young physicians entail possible hazards. However, Katarzyna is more likely to succeed in being a catalyst for change not only because of the esteem in which she is held as a medical professional, but because she has already learned how to become more inclusive in other ways.

> ### Example: Dinesh
>
> *Dinesh is a purchasing manager based in the high-tech city of Noida, India, close to Delhi. He has a reputation for being skilled at motivation, problem-solving, and hands-on instruction, which is exactly the right recipe for his relatively young team members. Dinesh has also built a strong network throughout the Noida site and with his counterparts at headquarters in London thanks to rotations through previous job assignments and a short expatriate stint at the worldwide purchasing department headquarters in the UK.*
>
> *Dinesh has noticed that women employees at his site tend to advance slowly, with men occupying most of the key management roles. Some managers have a tendency to "talk down" to their subordinates, especially women. There are also workplace cliques based on different linguistic, ethnic, and educational backgrounds within India that at times leave both men and women feeling isolated or left out of workplace conversations.*

It appears that assessment and development of talent are inconsistent at Dinesh's location, and that there may also be bias related to gender or other background factors. Dinesh has been considering several countermeasures that he personally could take, each of which will require some degree of courage on his part to go against current trends. On the other hand, during informal conversations he has had with managers who are his peers, several have agreed with his assessment and shared his willingness to promote changes. Dinesh has recently resolved to take three specific steps:

- Support high-potential women candidates during promotion discussions by providing examples of his interactions with them.

- Speak with one particular colleague he has observed "talking down" or appearing to demean others, finding a time for a private conversation to share his observations and to ask the colleague about his intent.

- Model outreach to employees from different backgrounds, not only on his own team but in the lunchroom, to diminish the potentially divisive influence of workplace cliques.

A Range of Options

Leading a systemic change effort will strike many people as a daunting and risky task. It is true that driving organizational change in areas such as the talent cycle requires political savvy, experience, and possibly seniority as well—not to mention a sustained commitment of energy. Serving as an inclusion champion, however, can take many forms, including small-scale everyday actions such as the final item on Dinesh's list above. The common expression, "See something, say something," may refer to an action taken by one individual who observes a micro-inequity that does not appear to be evident to the person who committed it. One-on-one comments, if made in a careful and considerate way, could result in a "thank you" rather than in the counterpart being offended or alienated:

- When you were texting during the meeting, did you notice how the others who were present reacted?

- I know that you were excited and wanted to contribute, but how do you think Sonya felt about the way that you interrupted her?

"Pick your battles" is probably good advice in deciding when to champion the cause of an inclusion effort or when to hold back. Returning to the theme of empathy highlighted in Chapter 5, one way we can choose how best to act is to get to know our colleagues well enough to discover what troubles or excites them, and then find ways to address occasions when they feel excluded. This could mean serving as a champion on a smaller scale or on a grander one, depending on how deep-rooted or systemic the underlying issue turns out to be. Daily acts of coaching, mentoring, or outreach to others have a cumulative impact. Another positive action is to note examples of inclusion as they occur and to spread these success stories to others; authentic local anecdotes make inclusivity seem more accessible.

"There is nobody at higher levels in this organization who looks like me."

"My team leader asked me to present to the executive team this time, and coached me on how to do it."

Becoming a Champion: Summary

The following list of recommendations includes a range of options from lower to higher risk and impact:

- **Ask colleagues** from different backgrounds how you can support them.

- **Mentor and coach others** with different backgrounds or styles; share the "unwritten rules" on how things are done in your organization.

- **Seek out mentors** who are different from you.

- **Adapt your leadership style** and give on-the-spot coaching and developmental support to people from different backgrounds; keep in mind different motivators and feedback approaches.

- Actively build a **work environment** of trust, respect, and psychological safety that enables people to speak up without fear of criticism or penalty.

- **Speak up!** Address the situation when a colleague makes an inappropriate comment or tells an offensive joke.

- **See something, say something**: Be alert for hurtful, disrespectful or unjust comments or decisions—either your own or those of others. Constructively address these to ensure that people can make amends and create a more inclusive environment.

- Brainstorm ways to keep the topic of inclusion dynamic and alive. **Be open to new approaches** - others are likely to see this and to feel more comfortable taking action themselves.

- **Create opportunities** for talented persons from diverse backgrounds to work on visible projects.

- **Advocate for highly capable people** from backgrounds different from your own, even when their styles are different from corporate culture norms. For example, when told that a person with a unique workstyle is "not ready" for a new assignment, important project or promotion, question the evaluation for bias.

- Be an **organizational change agent** when needed: Explain the business case for inclusion and serve as a role model in terms of inclusive behaviors. Address aspects of the talent life cycle (recruiting, engagement, performance assessment, rewards & retention, talent development), finding ways to make them more inclusive.

Inclusive Behavior #5: Getting Results

Leveraging diversity to innovate and to grow the business is the ultimate goal for most leaders who strive to be inclusive. Inclusive leadership can be justified in a broad moral and historical context as a matter of social justice, but organizations that answer to shareholders must naturally scrutinize any investments of time and resources for their practical efficacy—inclusion initiatives are no exception. Yet rhetoric about the effects of diversity on innovation is often not backed up by skilled innovation leadership and positive business results. How, specifically, can diversity be leveraged to achieve more effective performance, and where can it be an obstacle as well as an opportunity? Ultimately workplace inclusion needs to produce practical results or it will not be seen as a real business imperative.

Mitigating the potential risks of legal actions is of course a significant advantage in itself; exclusionary actions, even those that are unintended, can be costly, distracting, and damaging to employee engagement. Beyond the very real risks that need to be addressed, though, there are major opportunities as well. The following example demonstrates how inclusive leadership is likely to be an essential ingredient even for viable product development.

Example: Deion

Deion is a seasoned leader with a Fortune 100 manufacturer. He recently relocated to Singapore, far from his company's U.S. headquarters. His assignment is to head up a regional team that will take the lead globally in developing a new product for which the Asia-Pacific region is now the largest market.

Deion is a skilled listener and a veteran manager with a reputation for providing fair and balanced feedback. As an African-American, Deion thought that he was well aware of the meaning of diversity and inclusion, and had been an active leader in an employee resource group at an early stage in his career. Now in Singapore, given the unfamiliar diversity elements among local employees within his office, he has been feeling unsure about how to lead his team. He still feels culturally awkward, as he can spot unexpected reactions from his local colleagues, but doesn't yet fully understand what they are thinking and feeling. Nonetheless, he needs his team to deliver outstanding results.

Deion is in a new market with a new team. In order to lead his product development project successfully, he must cultivate a deep understanding of regional customer needs, competitors, supply chain capabilities, and the resources available within his own local organization. Although he is a company veteran with extensive engineering expertise and prior experience in this product line, trying to replicate what has previously worked in North America is unlikely to produce a good product fit for Asia-Pacific. There are substantial market differences, including the types of customer solutions the product must address, the most desirable features, the pace of development, local standards for the size of the product footprint, acceptable price points, financing arrangements, and expectations for follow-up service. Although Deion's team members regard him as an expert and are willing to follow his instructions, he is going to need to tap their expertise and insights from the very beginning of the project. Building upon other inclusive leadership behaviors discussed thus far, here are a few of the many steps that Deion could take to create an inclusive, high-performing team:

- Establish a diverse network of relationships, both with team members and across the regional organization, to build his knowledge about colleagues, the organization, and the market.

- Adapt his communication style to draw out ideas, to confirm understanding and/or agreement, and to read subtle messages from team members who prefer indirect communication methods.

- Learn how to inspire and elicit the best contributions of team members from different backgrounds based on deep understanding of their skills and potential.

- Leverage the knowledge of local team members to ensure that their insights into the needs of regional customers are accurately reflected in the product design.

- Balance customization that is truly required to meet unique local or regional needs with global standardization for maximum efficiency.

The need for a newly arrived expatriate such as Deion to be inclusive in order to achieve his team's objectives is relatively easy to perceive, although many international assignees actually do fail by ignoring local input and attempting to repeat past patterns of success in other markets without modification. Beyond the realm of expatriates, greater inclusiveness can enhance the quality and quantity of innovation organization-wide.

Innovation Cycle—Generate, Plan, Implement

Leaders of successful innovation efforts tap diverse perspectives and capabilities of team members through several stages of innovation: idea generation, planning, and implementation. Companies have various innovation platforms and processes, but all must traverse the broad path from divergence to convergence, or from early-stage ideation to go-to-market implementation.

Figure 6.2: Innovation Stages

Generate

During the idea generation stage of an innovation effort, diverse teams have the potential to perform in their full glory. They can accomplish this through a combination of all the stages of inclusive behaviors described in this chapter and in previous ones. Inclusive team leaders learn to systematically leverage the many perspectives that their team members offer, and to draw in even more when needed.

At the idea generation stage, a useful starting point is to have all team members consider who their normal "go-to people" are when they approach a problem likely to require an innovative solution. Once they have mapped the individuals to whom they turn most often, they can then analyze these contacts to consider how broad or narrow their reach might be. Team members are thereby able to determine how to broaden their network of contacts if needed to fulfill their objectives.

Inclusive leaders not only expand their team's network, but they also strive to seek out, filter, and incorporate fresh ideas in an objective manner. On an everyday basis, whether at home or abroad, there are frequently team members and other colleagues who have useful ideas to offer, but for some reason—communication style, gender, nationality, age—their potential contributions have been ignored or discounted.

The following anecdote describes an innovation leader who found that his organization was falling prey to a surprisingly regular form of unconscious bias against valuable engineering ideas, and sought to counteract this trend.

> ### Sourcing New Ideas
>
> *Wolfgang, a director for a large high technology company based in Europe, heard concerns expressed by a variety of people—customers, employees, fellow executives—that his organization was losing its innovative edge. Moreover, the*

> *company had made a strategic decision to expand its portfolio of product offerings for fast-growth markets in other regions. Employee survey results suggested that management practices might be an impediment to innovation. More specifically, there were comments that technical managers had been ignoring ideas from individuals whom they assumed were less qualified than others: "Our European engineers had a tendency to ignore the ideas of our engineers in India."*
>
> *Inspired by the practice of blind orchestra auditions, which has resulted in far more female musicians being selected for open orchestra positions when judges are unable to perceive gender based on appearance, Wolfgang instituted a blind audition process for new ideas. All participants in a company-wide drive to generate product improvement ideas received nicknames so that no one who was assessing the ideas could associate them with a particular region or country.*
>
> *The results of this relatively modest experiment were impressive. Far more ideas were selected and implemented from engineers outside of Europe than had previously been the norm. Wolfgang comments, "The new process made us see the possibility of innovation through diverse thought in our own organization. It made us listen to one another in new ways, without our normal filters, and it powered a real shift in the organization."*[1]

Plan

Once creative ideas have been generated, most teams go through a planning process that involves setting priorities and formulating a strategic plan. Edward de Bono became famous for his "Six Thinking

Hats" approach to developing ideas. He suggested that team members recognize the cognitive stance that they would normally take—passionate advocate (red hat), data-driven analyst (white hat), habitual critic (black hat), process controller (blue hat), etc.—and learn to wear these hats purposefully and in a collaborative manner.[2]

Beyond this valuable application of different cognitive styles to cultivate ideas, there are other useful filters which apply the "lenses" provided by different dimensions of diversity, such as generation, race and ethnicity, or gender (see Figure 6.3 below). For example, the automotive industry has become increasingly focused on the changing attitudes of a younger generation of consumers in the U.S. and Europe. In contrast to older drivers who took their driving tests on the first possible date of eligibility and for whom car ownership was a significant life milestone, younger consumers tend to be indifferent about car ownership, nervous about learning to drive, and more concerned than their elders about the dangers posed by distracted drivers. Automakers have unexpectedly discovered that certain autonomous vehicle features that they are testing—autonomous parking, lane control, blind spot sensors, automatic braking—can become attractive current selling features to these younger buyers who are accustomed to deploying high-tech fixes in other aspects of their lives, in contrast to their elders who probably retain the habit of looking over their shoulders when changing lanes. A fresh generational perspective has led automotive marketing and research and development teams to prioritize such features and to plan how to leverage their appeal to younger drivers.

Figure 6.3: Diversity Lenses

DIVERSITY LENSES
- Cognitive Style
- Generation
- Race & Ethnicity
- Gender
- Culture

Diverse teams often flounder when it comes time to hammer out and commit to a strategic plan in order to get things done. Would-be inclusive leaders often feel a gravitational pull toward complexity, ambiguity, and confusion—the natural outcome of having many different working styles and points of view. Leaders of high-performing global teams regularly consider several questions about their decision-making process that are highly inclusive, while remaining focused on business objectives and not just inclusion for its own sake:

- **What** information should we be looking at together?
- **Who** should be involved in this decision?
- **How** can we share ideas in a way that everyone is able to contribute?[3]

Using a disciplined process such as this one enables a team to continue to leverage its diverse resources but not be distracted by forces that will require it to go back to the beginning and start over. Even the classic Deming cycle of "plan—do—check—act" can go astray if it does not address these three questions. It is vital to define the breadth of information the team requires (the *What*) and the right people to engage in the planning process (the *Who*). Then, when the right people are together in the same physical or virtual space, it is just as important to have a process in place (the *How*) that enables everyone to express their points of view. Likewise, the team must have a clearly defined decision-making process—whether this is democratic, consultative, or directive—that enables it to move toward closure.

Implement

Tom Kelley of the renowned design firm Ideo wrote a book called *The Ten Faces of Innovation* in which he describes different roles people can take to move a project toward completion.[4] Inclusive leaders can also tap diverse team members for their particular skill sets or working styles in the implementation process. Members with specific functional skills can obviously contribute their specialized expertise in areas such as engineering, finance, or marketing. In a business environment where companies are vying for global innovation leadership, it is also worth considering, for instance, how the cultural profiles of different individuals could be utilized for the benefit of the team as a whole.

A team member who is status-oriented may have unique insights into customer expectations in a hierarchical society such as China or India, and could be designated as the "Master of Customer Care." Or to evaluate the pros and cons of product rollout timing options in different global markets, it might be useful to pair a more risk-oriented individual with a person who is more certainty-oriented. A relationship-oriented person from a culture where building amicable and trusting relationships is an art form could be designated as the "Teambuilder," while a task-focused team member could be assigned to some of the most time-sensitive deliverables as "The Enforcer." Such labels can be playful, intentional, and practically useful at the same time. They also help to keep the members of a heterogeneous team focused on implementation rather than reverting back to idea generation, which comes more easily.

The potential of a diverse workforce will only be fully unleashed when it is tapped to innovate and grow the business. This means far more than a rich brainstorming session which generates attractive ideas that then falter or fall flat when it comes to implementation. Managing global innovation means leveraging diversity from every possible angle to drive the innovation process all the way from inception to execution. This is easier said than done, but the steps outlined here—generate, plan, implement—provide a partial roadmap. Leaders who adopt these practices or invent their own methods for eliciting contributions from diverse team members will discover plenty of reasons to celebrate diversity.

Developing Future Leaders

Getting results means not only blending the best ideas from different sources to create superior products or services, but also recruiting, retaining, and developing a diverse array of leaders who can drive future growth. An important aspect of the talent life cycle depicted at the beginning of this chapter is discernment in evaluating future potential. We tend to look for ourselves in the mirror when identifying future leadership prospects, and this approach is fundamentally flawed in organizations with a diverse global workforce.

Sometimes the source of bias is primarily linguistic. People may be promoted into leadership roles because they have the language skills to communicate well with executives, but lack technical capabilities, customer knowledge, or the respect of fellow employees. In other cases employees might be misjudged, for example, based on more deep-rooted racial, ethnic, gender, or cultural biases that shape the conclusion: "This person is just not leadership material." Current leaders who implement an

open-minded and insightful approach to evaluating talent are generally both welcomed by employees and respected for doing the right thing for the business:

> *Recently a new global leader who is very good at judging people took over our line of business. It was so exciting to see her listen carefully to each person on her team, speak to other employees, and go on customer visits, even when she had to communicate mostly through an interpreter. We gradually began to open up and tell her who is really capable, and she has begun to promote those people, including one local salesperson who doesn't speak other languages well but has won a lot of business with customers and is very much respected by employees.[5]*

Once high-potential talent has been identified, leaders must be able to follow up with flexible developmental practices that may differ from their own preferred norms. For example, a manager who is normally hands-off—"I hate to be micromanaged myself and imagine that others dislike this as well"—might discover that a hands-on style is required with a promising team member. Standard delegation practices that work in one environment could be regarded critically as "delegate and disappear" in another. The emerging patterns of leadership exhibited by employees based on their own distinctive life experiences may be both unexpected and unlike those of executives who were previously held up as role models. As one respected leader comments, "I had to give others the chance to prove themselves successful in ways that no one had been successful before, and to utilize their own values and styles to be successful."

Inclusive leadership development thus produces several kinds of positive outcomes. Employees are open in sharing their best ideas, customers are well-served, and high-potential employees are retained and ready for future assignments with augmented responsibilities. Beyond these effects, close relationships with a diverse range of employees can provide current leaders themselves with valuable feedback and a level of commitment and performance that is otherwise difficult to achieve: "If you are honest with people and show them you are trying to help their career, they will give you everything they've got."[6]

> **Getting Results: Summary**
>
> - **Proactively seek out ideas**, approaches and perspectives from people who do not think like you do. Express appreciation for their input, even when you disagree.
>
> - **Explore the suggestions of others** before introducing your own proposals.
>
> - **Seek out internal and external customers** that you could learn more about in order to understand their needs deeply, tapping the insights of employees whose backgrounds are similar to those of the customers.
>
> - **Experience unfamiliar markets directly** by sampling competitors' products, living in a local residence, riding the subway, or spending a week in the factory.
>
> - **Consider the blind solicitation of new ideas** to ensure that proposals are judged on their own merits. Be alert to new ways of achieving results and solving problems.
>
> - Learn to distinguish between **real agreement and polite responses** that do not signify understanding or commitment.
>
> - Establish processes that enable team members to **analyze challenges from various angles** and to build new ideas or proposed solutions together, using relevant diversity lenses.
>
> - **Examine workplace habits or systems that may benefit from inclusion.** Check "the What, the Who, and the How" of key team processes. What changes could bring improved results?

- **When making decisions**, allow time for consultation and meeting preparation. This fosters more open discussions and allows for the expression of differing opinions.

- **Be a catalyst for team solutions** by taking a joint problem-solving approach that encourages others to think together rather than to debate as adversaries. Find the best solutions by integrating multiple sources.

- Continue to **leverage diverse team member backgrounds during the implementation phase**, considering their cultural profiles when determining key roles.

- **View the talent life cycle as an additional means of producing results**. Are you looking for yourself in the mirror or are you willing to sponsor leaders with different backgrounds and styles?

- **Make a genuine commitment to developing the careers of others** with leadership potential, even if they have a radically different style compared to yours.

- **Be prepared to modify your developmental approach** to high-potential employees based on their real needs.

- **Seek feedback** on the efficacy of your own leadership style so that you can continue to develop in addition to developing others.

CHAPTER SEVEN

Brain-Based Leadership: What's Missing?

What are the value and limits of current neuroscience-based approaches to inclusion and diversity?

Approaches to leadership based on neuroscience are alluring. Advances in functional magnetic resonance imaging (fMRI) have provided an exciting new window into the everyday workings of the brain. Consultants and coaches eagerly cite the latest neuroscience research as the basis for their leadership advice, focusing on how it can be applied to vital tasks such as driving a successful change initiative.

And what could be a more common human asset than the brain, with its magnificent synapses and plasticity as well as its flaws?

> Numerous costly failures, including cross-border acquisitions, change initiatives, and rollouts of well-intended inclusion and diversity efforts can be traced to cultural blindness.

Brain-based leadership development seems sensible, scientific, and compelling, with the potential for global applications that bridge pesky nuances, paradoxes, and differences.

What could possibly be missing?

Before jumping on this popular bandwagon, let's explore factors that comprise a full human being and contribute to successful leadership. Here's an example:

> *Albert Farnsworth was a fast-rising leader from the UK assigned to run a firm in Hong Kong that his company had recently acquired. Confident in his prior leadership track record, primarily from his work in northern Europe, and armed with the advice of a U.K.-based coach informed by neuroscience research, he developed a plan for integrating the new acquisition.*

> Albert sought to reduce status threats related to the acquisition by demonstrating respect for the status of the firm's previous leaders. He preserved their titles, assigning to himself the newly-coined title of managing director. In his usual egalitarian style, he frequently asked local managers and employees for their input on key decisions, with brainstorming sessions designed to draw out their ideas. He sought to preserve employees' sense of autonomy and certainty by establishing broad goals for the organization and then giving them room to create their own solutions—this was a leadership style that had worked well for him in the past and had been a key part of his own success story to date. He also began to introduce them to their new matrix counterparts around the world, stressing how the new parent company's relatively flat hierarchy enabled the best ideas to move quickly between regions.
>
> Unfortunately, the plan did not generate the results that Albert had anticipated. Both sales and morale began to drop, his team brainstorming sessions seemed to go nowhere, and soon key junior employees began leaving the firm, hired away by local companies. When Albert asked his local HR manager for results from employee exit interviews, he was unpleasantly surprised by the criticisms of his own leadership, expressed in comments such as the following:
>
> - "We don't know who the boss is anymore. Our previous leaders didn't perform well and that is why they had to sell the company. Now they are stuck in the middle between us and Albert, and don't know what to do."
> - "Albert is always asking for our opinions, which makes us think that he doesn't know what he is doing and is a weak leader."

> - "He seems to delegate and disappear. We want someone we can bring problems to and then solve them together."
> - "We want more change and faster. The market is moving very rapidly here, and the new boss should fire older managers who can't keep up."

Albert's primary failing and one that almost derailed his career was his attempt to replicate his prior success by using the same leadership style in a different cultural environment. In this case, his application of neuroscience to address the importance of status issues during the ownership transition contributed to overconfidence in his plan and actually reinforced his cultural blindness rather than providing him with contextually appropriate leadership strategies.

Brain-Based Leadership: The Missing Hemisphere

There have been various critiques of neuroscience-based leadership approaches and their skillful branding, which includes the display of colorful brain models and fMRI images at training events to highlight their scientific aura. Warren Bennis, a well-known pioneer in the field of leadership development, noted that much of this new movement repackages prior insights, especially those of Daniel Goleman on emotional intelligence. He states, "What worries me is people being taken in by the language of it and ending up with stuff we've known all along."[1]

Although such comments raise concerns, there is arguably a *deeper* problem with neuroscience-based leadership approaches that has not received sufficient attention. Their universal claims and attractive packaging can reinforce a convenient "one size fits all" solution for leadership development across global organizations. Such standardized solutions are usually ethnocentric, reinforcing the impulse to evaluate others based on our own standards and to make "them" more like "us"; this becomes even easier to justify with a seemingly invincible scientific rationale to back it up.

The core problem with the current applications of neuroscience to leadership is not that they are wrong, but that they are incomplete, unbalanced, and potentially misleading. It turns out that there is a lot more evidence available, including research from additional branches of neuroscience, that can help provide a fuller picture of humanity with vital implications for leadership.

Nature and Nurture

Anyone who studied Psychology 101 in college during the past fifty years was likely introduced to the nature vs. nurture debate. Simply put, research indicates that **human beings are products of both their genetic makeup (nature) and their physical and cultural environments (nurture).**

In fact, a key differentiator of humans from other species is that they are *less* genetically pre-programmed (nature) and *more* responsive to novel or changing environmental factors (nurture). Humans develop from childhood based on cultural influences such as how they are held, whom they live with, where they sleep, what they eat, the sounds they hear, the stories they are told, the ways in which they are praised or scolded, and so on. One definition of culture is that it is a way of addressing common human challenges in a particular environment. Each culture passes on the successful survival methods of its elders that fit a distinctive time and place, and these learnings shape the way that each brain is configured.

To date, neuroscience-based leadership approaches have focused primarily on the "nature" side of nature/nurture equation, highlighting common features of human physiology and cognitive functioning, while generally ignoring the "nurture" or environmental component, which plays an equally powerful role in shaping human development. **Culture is too often treated cheerfully as an organizational feature to be "built" or "redefined"** based on scientific insights into the brain, **rather than as a pervasive developmental**

influence that shapes the very functioning of the brain itself in different ways, depending upon our upbringing.

Culture and the Brain: Research Examples

There are a number of studies commonly neglected by current neuroscience leadership gurus that provide fascinating and important evidence for how human brains can be wired differently based on cultural influences.

Study #1: Does Self Refer to "Me" or "We"?

The prefrontal cortex region of the brain is believed to represent our idea of the self. One research study found that this area became active when U.S. study participants thought of their own personal identities and traits. For Chinese study participants, on the other hand, this region was activated by adjectives describing both themselves and their mothers.[2] In other words, the very **definition of self is shaped by culture**. Different definitions of "me" or "we" can and do lead to very different leadership styles.

Study #2: Attention to Objects vs. Context

Another study revealed distinctly different attentional bias based on culture. This study showed sample images to both Western and East

Asian participants. Westerners, whose cultures place a high value on independence and individuality, tended to focus their attention on particular foreground objects, with less regard for context and relationships among items.

In contrast, East Asian participants, whose cultures emphasize interdependent relationships and awareness of context, focused their attention on the context of the image and demonstrated relational processing of information.[3]

So not only our self-definition but also **what we pay attention to is culturally influenced**. Leaders from varied cultural backgrounds may notice quite different things, with some focusing on the action items in the foreground, and others examining the broader context.

Study #3: Valuing "Modesty" or "Assertiveness"

A third study found that the area of the brain that produces dopamine, or the "feel-good hormone," responds differently based on cultural conditioning. The study showed volunteers from the U.S. and Japan drawings of a person standing in a relatively submissive pose, with head down and shoulders hunched, and of another person standing in a more dominant pose, with arms crossed and face forward.

Respondents interpreted the same pictures differently based on their cultural values. Japanese participants produced dopamine when viewing the first drawing, as they interpreted the submissive posture positively, seeing it as a demonstration of modesty and respect. U.S. participants produced dopamine when viewing the second drawing, as they saw the dominant pose as an indication of confidence and strength.[4]

How we define ourselves, what we perceive, and the judgments we make are all shaped by our cultural environments...

Implications for Leaders

These three studies and others like them from the **emerging field of "cultural neuroscience"** have enormous implications for the development of leaders on a global scale. To avoid becoming the latest form of ethnocentrism, dressed up this time in white lab coats, brain-based leadership approaches must embrace both nature *and* nurture to help leaders work effectively around the world.

If how we define ourselves, what we perceive, and the judgments we make are all shaped by our cultural environments, leaders need to understand both what makes them similar to *and* what makes them different from their global colleagues. They must also cultivate skills for adapting to each other in integrated global workplaces that could involve virtual meetings, travel to distant locations, or working with a diverse mix of colleagues in the same building.

Approaches to leadership informed by neuroscience are incomplete if they fail to take into account not only how the brain functions but also the cultural influences that shape it. What are the implications of a more holistic view of the brain, encompassing both "nature" and "nurture," for leadership development?

Culture and Leadership: The Missing Hemisphere

Consider the SCARF model described by David Rock, head of the NeuroLeadership Institute and author of *Your Brain at Work*. Although the five elements of this model—Status, Certainty, Autonomy, Relatedness, and Fairness—are convincingly linked with research into fundamental brain functions such as our "fight or flight" impulses, all of these elements are also subject to culturally based indoctrination and interpretation. It would be a mistake to assume that each SCARF element manifests itself similarly everywhere, or that the model can applied to promote **"culture change" without cultural understanding**.

For example, while it is true that Status, the "S" in SCARF, is important everywhere, this aspect of human behavior is expressed and interpreted quite differently based on particular environmental contexts. Some cultures are far more hierarchical than others, and hierarchy is also manifested in different ways. In China, for instance, it is relatively common to have a person who is clearly in the role of the **"boss"** issuing orders in a directive style, while many U.S. and northern European organizations attempt to distribute significant authority to other leadership team members and throughout the organization, endorsing **"leadership at all levels."**

So in one cultural environment, the greatest perceived threat could be having a leader who is overly directive, violating others' sense of status, while in another it might be having no boss or unclear lines of authority. In the case of Albert Farnsworth, by attempting to drive change in his new environment using his own culturally conditioned approach to status—delegating authority to local leaders, engaging in regular brainstorming sessions, and introducing local employees to their global matrix counterparts—the result was confusion and disengagement rather than effective "culture change."

As generations of expatriates have discovered at great cost, culture change is possible within an organization or team with sustained focus over time, but only based on deep knowledge of the broader national cultural environment—and woe to those who embark on a mission to change the whole country. Through the mental lens of Albert's relatively hierarchical, group-oriented local employees in Hong Kong, and in contrast to his self-image as a skillful facilitator and change agent, Albert appeared instead to be a weak and uncertain leader who failed to make decisive changes while preferring to "delegate and disappear."

Status can even take on different, complex forms based on national and organizational cultures that frequently harbor contradictions. Many companies in the U.S. pride themselves on their egalitarian cultures and informal styles, while still taking for granted executive compensation that may be as much as 900 times the median employee salary. Major differences can also exist among generations, regions, functions, genders, and socioeconomic classes within the same country.

In Albert's new Hong Kong-based acquisition, it turned out that generational differences were critically important. The most senior managers whose own parents had known great hardship and social chaos (many were refugees from China's civil war and the Cultural Revolution) valued the respect for their status offered by an unchanged job title as well as continuity with previous policies. Meanwhile, employees in the same workplace from a younger millennial generation were more accustomed to prosperity, social stability, and constant opportunities for growth. Many of these employees were far less attached to the status quo and more ready to embrace change, expressing impatience at Albert's slow pace in moving conservative senior leaders out of the way. ("After all, they are the ones who failed and had to sell the company.") For these younger employees, his demonstration of respect for the status of senior local managers was misplaced, and quickly became a source of frustration and disengagement.

What is true for Status also holds for any other aspect of the SCARF model—universal human traits are molded by one's physical environment and cultural upbringing, and are expressed in workplaces around the world in ways that are both similar and different. The SCARF model highlights what we need to pay attention to, but not necessarily how to adapt our approach to fit different global environments. **Leaders ignore culture at their peril, including the nuances and differences within cultures as well as among them**. Numerous costly failures, including cross-border acquisitions, change initiatives, and rollouts of well-intended inclusion and diversity efforts ("Gender issues are the same everywhere, right?") can be traced to cultural blindness.

Cultural Differences: Five Dimensions

Each of the cultural dimensions depicted in Figure 7.1 below represents a spectrum of behavior that varies based on cultural context.

These dimensions of culture overlap with four out of five elements of the SCARF model:

- *Status:* Egalitarianism/Status
- *Certainty*: Risk/Certainty
- *Autonomy*: Independent/Interdependent
- *Relatedness*: Task/Relationship

Such dimensions highlight contrasts among national cultures that have been borne out by decades of research, including data from hundreds of thousands of survey respondents. National cultures may change over time, but the process is generally slow and uneven, and can result in either convergence or divergence in comparison with other national norms. The ways in which people actually behave along each of these dimensions are influenced by their own dynamic cultural settings just as they are by the structure of the brain—in fact, these two pervasive influences on human behavior are closely intertwined.

Figure 7.1: Dimensions of National Culture

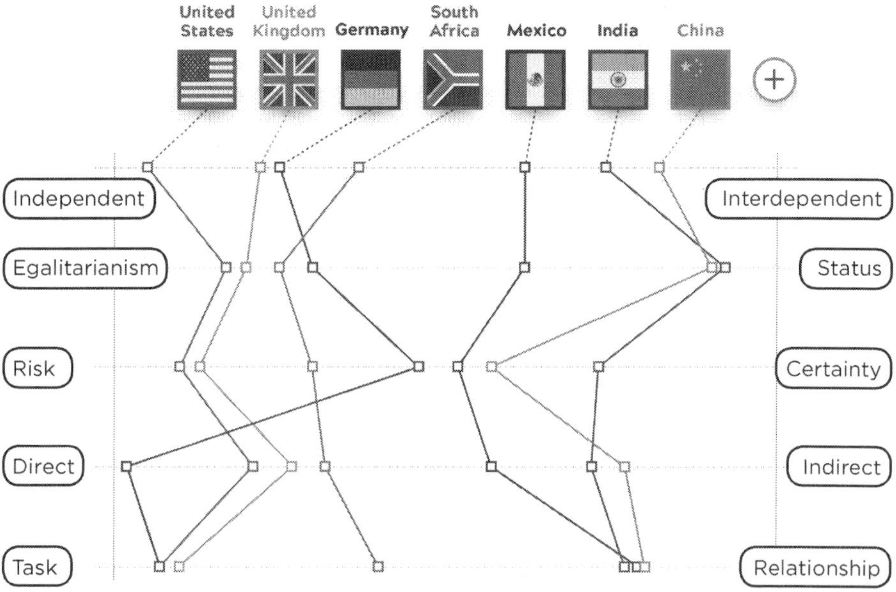

Leadership Development: Implications

So what are the implications of the "nurture" side of the nature/nurture equation for leadership development? There is of course value to **current neuroscience-based approaches** if they are used wisely, based on the knowledge that they address one part of the leadership development picture and are not a panacea. When used exclusively, however, particularly in a global leadership context, they **can be readily classified as fitting either the "Denial" or "Minimization" phases of the intercultural development scale** that charts movement from a monocultural, or ethnocentric, mindset, to an intercultural mindset.[5]

The stages in this scale, themselves derived from extensive research, are Denial, Polarization, Minimization, Acceptance, and Adaptation. Leadership approaches that focus on human similarities while consistently underestimating differences cannot support progress toward the more advanced stages of this intercultural developmental spectrum. Approaches grounded in the brain's physiology often tell us that our brains perceive "difference" as a potential threat, but give us inadequate guidance for how to adapt. **Full understanding of the power of culture requires a pragmatic embrace of both similarities and differences.**

Figure 7.2: Intercultural Development Continuum

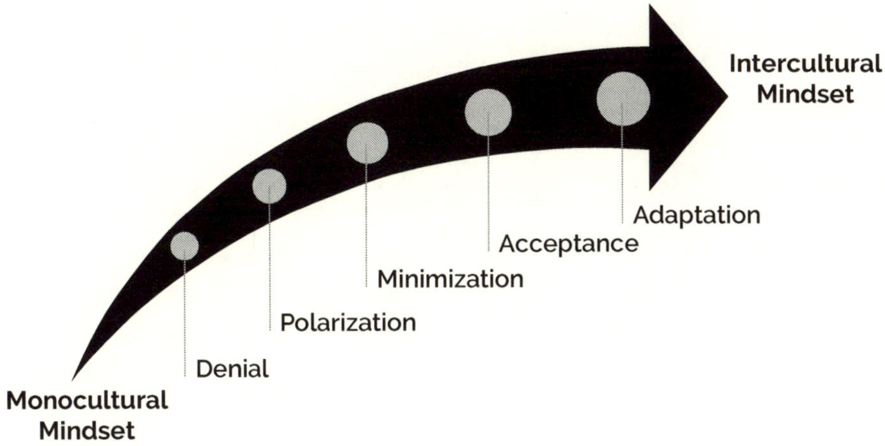

Monocultural Mindset → Denial → Polarization → Minimization → Acceptance → Adaptation → Intercultural Mindset

Holistic approaches to neuroscience and leadership development will incorporate both nature and nurture, or brain physiology and culture. Current and future global leaders need to cultivate knowledge and skills that include:

- Personality *and* cultural self-awareness—personal characteristics as well as culturally based assumptions

- Psychological *and* cultural neuroscience—common features of the human brain as well as the developmental effects of different cultural contexts that also influence how humans behave

- Culture change *and* cultural influence—how to change culture in comparatively small-scale settings (particularly organizational and team cultures) while at the same time recognizing the pervasive influence of national cultures (transmitted via families, schools, and workplaces) on our behavior

A balanced approach to leadership development includes deliberately paradoxical terms such as "adaptive authenticity," acknowledging the need to work with both what we are given and who we can become. Leaders must draw upon their own upbringing and core values while being deliberately open to "mind-blowing" experiences with colleagues from different backgrounds that could change them forever. This approach is flexible and open-ended, acknowledging that **successful leaders can and do accomplish tasks very differently, and that there are various ways to inspire colleagues and to solve problems effectively in different environments**.

One-size-fits-all approaches to leadership development in any form are alluring but ultimately bound to run squarely into their own limitations. Even attractive and modern-sounding packages such as neuroscience-based leadership can prove lopsided and therefore circumscribed in their usefulness unless they embrace how human beings are both fundamentally similar and profoundly different.

CHAPTER EIGHT

Regional Inclusion Challenges

 *Are inclusion challenges the same everywhere, or are there differences across regions such as Asia-Pacific, EMEA, or North America?*

Leaders who encounter employees or customers behaving in unfamiliar ways need to understand "the why behind the behavior." Such understanding is essential to begin to motivate, to sell, and to shrink the common gap between what we intend and the

> Efforts to establish common organizational goals, principles, and standards of conduct are feasible if they are adapted based on local knowledge.

impact that our actions have. For leaders who interact with a diverse range of employees, globally or domestically, it is important to understand the differences among and even within countries.

For example, **women** are underrepresented in leadership positions worldwide, but this is particularly true in Asia-Pacific. A McKinsey study notes,

> *Worldwide, slightly less than four women hold leadership positions for every ten men in business and politics. In Asia-Pacific, there is only one woman in leadership positions for every four men. In some countries in East Asia, there are only 12 to 20 women leaders for every 100 men.*[1]

Women across Asia face a daunting combination of obstacles depending on the location, including educational discrimination; threats to physical safety; social norms regarding work after childbirth and the role of men in child-rearing; limited childcare options and the perception that children are better cared for by family members. They also encounter workplace stereotypes that women are best suited to particular industries such as consumer goods, retail, or hospitality; lack of female executive role models; business entertainment settings that may exclude women; and invisible ceilings in many organizations that limit women's advancement to higher roles.

In Europe, although gender issues are also common, **ageism** is an increasingly critical theme and is likely to become more important due to demographic trends. In a comprehensive survey of 55,000 people from 28 European countries, more than a third of respondents representing all age groups reported seeing unfair treatment based on age. The rapidly ageing workforce across most of Europe ensures that heightened sensitivity to age-based issues will continue for some time. The current ratio of four people of working age to each person over 65 will change to a ratio of just two to one by 2050, portending a growing burden on social services. In Europe, age discrimination is reportedly experienced more often than other forms of discrimination based on gender or race, and is a frequent source of workplace disputes. "Older people are likely to be stereotyped as warm but incompetent, feeding low expectations and lack of inclusion."[2]

Sub-Saharan Africa is a huge region comprising 46 of the continent's 54 countries and over a billion people. In spite of vast changes as cities expand and economies modernize, the legacy of colonialism lives on in many places. Tribal and ethnic differences formerly aggravated by colonial masters attempting to extend and maintain control have made it difficult for many countries to unify their citizens and to ensure orderly transitions of power.[3] In addition to armed conflicts and genocide in places like Sudan and Rwanda, or election-related violence in Kenya, for example, such rivalries influence conduct in some contemporary workplaces in less lethal but nonetheless significant forms. An employee may be afforded a position of prestige or looked down upon—even threatened—depending on tribal affiliation. As one expatriate living outside of his native Somalia reports, "It was a relief for me to move to another country because at home people looked at what I did based on the tribe I came from, and when I made a decision that went against the interests of another tribe, I felt that both me and my family were threatened."

Three Country Examples

Each country around the world faces its own unique constellation of inclusion challenges at the same time that it shares common themes with other locations. Here are a few examples that help to illustrate country-specific patterns and their implications for corporate inclusion initiatives:

Ghana

This West African nation of approximately 30 million people is well-known for its relative prosperity and democratic governance. It shares some characteristics with its near neighbors, but is distinguished from them in other ways—for example, Ghana is an anglophone country, with English as its official language and spoken by more than two-thirds of the population, surrounded by francophone neighbors: the Ivory Coast, Togo, and Burkina Faso.

Like its neighbors, Ghana contains a mix of ethnic groups, with over one hundred along with many languages, including 11 that are government-sponsored. The country's main ethnic groups are the Akan, representing almost half of the population, the Mole-Dagbon, Ewe, Ga-Dangme, and Gurma. Although employees in the workplace are often aware of the tribal backgrounds of their co-workers, and tribal references are common, these are comparatively less significant than in other locations on the continent, often taking the form of casual banter. As the majority ethnic group, the Akans, and especially the Ashantis, their largest subgroup—with their numbers and the proud history of the Ashanti kingdom—can be perceived as feeling superior.

Social distinctions that are still quite clear in Ghana are usually based on education and socioeconomic class. English language fluency is viewed as an indicator of educational background, and in spite of Ghana's overall literacy rate of 85 percent, levels of education vary widely from the elite with advanced technical degrees to members of less wealthy socioeconomic classes who may have the equivalent of a junior high school education. The striking gap between rich and poor can be seen on the same city block, with high tea served on the finest china to nattily attired guests on the upper floor of

---

Social distinctions that are still quite clear in Ghana are usually based on education and socioeconomic class.

---

an office building, while street vendors with dubious hygiene and wearing makeshift clothing sell products on the street below. Workplace opportunities are influenced by political, familial, or religious ties. Even extended family connections—including distant cousins or in-laws—carry considerable weight, as do school networks. Nepotism and cronyism are widespread, and sometimes even expected by members of the same group. The majority of Ghana's population is Christian, with a Muslim minority of less than 20 percent. Church elders, clergy, and other leaders are generally held in high esteem. However incongruous or inappropriate it might appear to Western organizations accustomed to separating religion from the workplace, successful social and corporate initiatives may partner with religious groups and incorporate religious values.

In white-collar workplace settings in Ghana, the people with whom local employees may feel the greatest tension are foreign expatriates whose hefty pay packages are seen as exceeding the value of their contribution. However, Ghana also has a relatively large number of economic migrants and illegal immigrants living within its borders. Estimates range widely, with the Ghana Immigration Service stating that immigrants number 14.6 percent of the total population, and are generally higher than the percentage of immigrants in European countries where this topic has been the source of controversy and political upheaval. Among other groups, an estimated one million Nigerians have immigrated to Ghana, and they are often accused of criminal activity, including internet-based fraud. Both Ghana and Nigeria have previously engaged in mass deportations of each other's citizens, depending on the economic climate of the times. Many Nigerians in Ghana complain that they are unfairly treated, being

forced to close their shops and experiencing everyday discrimination in workplaces or on the streets.[4] The size and growth rate of Nigeria's population, which is now estimated to be approximately 200 million, or more than six times the number of Ghanaians, suggests that the interactions between the citizens of the two countries will only become more frequent.[5]

Men in Ghana generally have greater social privileges than women country-wide, with women confronting an array of barriers stemming from their social context. Women in the workplace are often called upon to carry out domestic-type chores such as fetching food or drinks, and may not be included or heeded in strategic meetings. Ambitious, competitive women are maligned and accused of having risen through providing sexual favors. There are relatively low numbers of women in executive or management roles. Sexual harassment in the form of *quid pro quo*, or the demand for sexual favors in exchange even for overseeing apprenticeships or administering standard functions such as tests, is currently in Ghana's public eye based on a recent high-profile incident.[6] Harassment also takes place in more pervasive, everyday forms such as lewd remarks made to women by men who might actually be surprised to find that these are considered objectionable.

Inclusion in Ghana: Implications

Initiatives that address socioeconomic differences and the roles of women in the workplace are likely to have the most immediate relevance in addressing common sources of exclusion. Companies may want to consider providing supplementary education and training for those who have not benefited from elite higher education opportunities. Efforts to extend Western sexual harassment standards will appear relevant if they make connections with local examples; "quid pro quo" harassment can be readily explained, but comments and conduct defined elsewhere as creating a "climate of harassment" might not be regarded in the same way by men or even by some women, so the starting point for training efforts may need to be different.

What Does it Mean to be African?

Beginning in 2035, the number of young people reaching working age in Africa will exceed that of the rest of the world combined, and this trend will continue every year for the rest of the century. By 2050, one in every four humans will be African, and at the end of the century Africans will comprise 40 percent of the world's total population.[7] Five of the world's fastest-growing countries in terms of population range from west to east and north to south on the continent and include Nigeria, Ethiopia, Tanzania, Uganda, and the Democratic Republic of the Congo. Growth like this, along with its economic and humanitarian implications, makes it essential to reexamine previous images and stereotypes.

Africa is geographically larger than China, India, the contiguous U.S., and most of Europe combined. Cultural differences among Africans include religion, with adherents of Christianity—Protestant and Catholic—and Islam, as well as a variety of indigenous religions. There are also well-known differences between the anglophone and francophone regions of sub-Saharan Africa based on the legacy of colonialism, but differences among Africans go far deeper.

The African continent has over 3,000 ethnic groups and its people speak two thousand languages. The incredible variety of African geography—mountains, desert, jungle, savannah—has shaped a genetic diversity among people within Africa that is said to be greater than the genetic differences between Europeans and Chinese. Because humans originated in Africa, human beings have had more time to adapt there than anywhere else in the world.[8] There are Africans from every major racial group, with hundreds of millions of Arab North Africans from Morocco to Egypt, and even roughly one million Chinese who have arrived as expatriates, laborers, or immigrants.

At least 180 million members of the African diaspora, including first generation African emigrants, live around the world in North America, the Caribbean, Central America, Europe, and Asia. People of African heritage living abroad have taken on other genetic and cultural characteristics. Black Africans in the U.S. reportedly have an average of 25 percent white genetic heritage, reflecting in part centuries of exploitation as slaves. Skin pigmentation among African-Americans with this genetic mix is largely a matter of random variation—among children from the same set of parents, one may appear "white" and the other "black." Self-concept and identity across Africans of all backgrounds vary considerably as well: African-Americans traveling to Africa sometimes report being surprised that at the same time they may have looked down on their African counterparts as residents of less developed countries, those same counterparts saw them as less than fully African.

In the broadest sense, all of humanity originated in Africa—we are all Africans—and Africa's burgeoning population will exert an increasingly large influence worldwide through economic growth, migration, conflict, consumption, culture, and the sheer vitality of the most youthful population on earth.

Germany

Germany is the largest member country of the European Union, with a population of 82 million. It has the world's fourth largest economy in terms of GDP, and a highly skilled workforce. The country also has an ageing population—with a median age of 47, Germany is the third oldest nation in the world, behind only Monaco and Japan (compared, for instance, with 38 for the U.S., 37 for China, 28 for India, and 18 for Nigeria).[9] Germany's population was previously predicted to decline to 68 million because of its low birth rate, and had actually begun to decrease year over year. Now, due to higher immigration levels and a slight birth-rate increase, the population could remain relatively stable going forward.[10]

A long-term demographic transformation has been taking place in Germany which had its roots in the labor shortage of the post-WWII years. Guest worker programs were put in place to address this shortfall, and many immigrant laborers later became permanent residents. Since West Germany's reunification with East Germany in 1990, and the dissolution of the Soviet Union in 1991, several million ethnic Germans from other former Eastern Bloc countries have also exercised their right to return to Germany. The establishment of the EU in 1993 allowed citizens from any EU country to work in other member states, causing additional economic migrants from EU nations to seek work in relatively prosperous nations like Germany where job opportunities are available.

At this point, Germany has the highest ever number of foreign citizens within its borders, with 10.6 million people, or more than 12% of the total population. Half of these are from EU states, and

---

Germany has the highest ever number of foreign citizens within its borders, with 10.6 million people, or more than 12% of the total population.

---

the other half are from elsewhere. Most recently, over 1.6 million asylum-seeking refugees, primarily from the Middle East and Africa, have entered the country just since 2014.[11] Germany now contains a wide array of ethnic minorities, including more than 2.8 million Turks along with large numbers of Poles, Russians, Italians, Syrians, and Africans from various nations. The recent spike in immigration has led to increased political tension, with nationalist, anti-immigration candidates garnering more votes and representation in the German federal parliament.

The combination of a high-tech economy, an ageing workforce, and large numbers of recent immigrants makes the transfer of knowledge and skills a crucial issue in German enterprises. As in other parts of Europe, the issue of age discrimination has received growing attention as well. The physical demands of manufacturing jobs in particular become more stressful and difficult for those increasing in age, and this is sometimes seen as an intractable problem and a reason to lower expectations for worker output, slow down manufacturing lines, or even close down some facilities with ageing workforces. Here is an example of how one leadership team attempted to address its workforce challenges by utilizing the unique capabilities of its older workers.

> ### Silver to Gold
>
> *The executives running a factory based near Munich, in German's southern state of Bavaria, were proud of their site's reputation for high quality and an extremely productive workforce. However, with many experienced older workers now retiring or approaching retirement age, they faced a two-fold onboarding problem.*
>
> *First, the learning curve of newly appointed team leaders in the factory had proved to be time-consuming and inefficient. Because of the inexperience of these new leaders, for example, they would typically follow a very rigid, by-the-book*

process whenever non-planned events such as a minor quality glitch or mechanical issue would emerge. The procedures for addressing these events were complex and time-consuming, resulting in lengthy, detailed reports, some of which were unnecessary.

In addition, the factory had also just voluntarily accepted a contingent of Middle Eastern refugees into its vocational training program. This was a highly visible project, and the initial interactions between these refugees and the workers assigned to train them had been more difficult than expected. After a short initial honeymoon period, poor communication and misunderstandings had led to increasing tensions, and the new employees were falling behind on their training milestones.

Based on extensive consultation with its Works Council, the factory's leadership instituted a new "Turning Silver into Gold" policy that paired experienced senior coaches/mentors with younger team leaders and with small groups of refugees. The experienced workers, who had no direct reporting line to either group, were able to help their younger team leader colleagues to better

prioritize their activities. Rather than blindly implementing standard procedures, the team leaders learned to implement quality control measures more selectively and efficiently. As these junior leaders began to appreciate the expertise and experience that the senior workers brought to them, they became eager to reach out and ask for their input.

Likewise, with more focused, hands-on attention, the refugee trainees' pace of learning began to accelerate as well. The older coaches/mentors were sufficiently enthusiastic that they collaborated to create an accelerated onboarding process for workers who often brought skills of their own but lacked previous vocational training in manufacturing. They also made an effort to get to know each of the new arrivals on a personal level to better understand their backgrounds and interests, and implemented meeting best practices to ensure that the trainees, none of whom were fluent in German, were able to understand detailed technical explanations and to ask questions.

The positive energy generated by this initiative during its implementation was enormous, with visible relief for overburdened team leaders and for refugees trying hard to succeed in their new roles. Factory leaders realized that they were in the midst of a large-scale knowledge transfer to younger team leaders and to their newest employees only made possible through valuing senior expertise. They had underestimated the subtle "tacit" knowledge and judgment that older factory workers had acquired through long hands-on experience. Greater inclusion of senior workers and their expertise in turn made the factory more inclusive of its newest entrants. This effort was so successful that even the local factory vice president requested a personal coach/mentor.

Ironically, a major challenge that those running this initiative faced in expanding it to other parts of

> the company was to advocate for its importance in comparison with other company inclusion measures already in place related to gender and disabilities. Eventually, a regional inclusion initiative leveraging senior worker experience was launched, building on the positive energy and the precedent established within this plant.

Inclusion in Germany: Implications

Inclusion of senior workers may need to be weighed as a corporate priority in addition to other important goals. Experienced workers have both knowledge and the capacity for judgment that will likely need to be conveyed in a hands-on manner rather than solely through documentation. Certain types of initiatives can be undertaken only through extensive consultation with enterprise-based Work Councils, but those entities can also be helpful in getting workers on board. Framing the contribution of older workers as "knowledge transfer" and/or "mentoring" could serve as one way to position such an effort positively for everyone involved.

The United States

The U.S. continues to struggle with its historical legacies of slavery and immigration. Race, gender, and illegal immigration are all sensitive, hot-button topics that must be handled with care. Federal law—in many cases augmented by state laws—prohibits discrimination against a broad list of "protected classes," or groups of people who are protected from employment discrimination based on race, color, religion, sex, age, disability, national origin, or veteran status. Alleged violations can result in major lawsuits against employers, incurring substantial legal costs and sometimes much larger expenses for settlements or penalties.

In addition to these legally protected categories, there has also been a renewed recognition that income and social class matter as well. Income distribution, drug addiction rates, voting patterns, and levels of access to medical care all appear to diverge along class lines. These trends affect educational opportunities, too. Children from economically disadvantaged backgrounds attend top universities at strikingly low rates: "At 38 colleges in America, including five in the Ivy League—Dartmouth, Princeton, Yale, Penn, and Brown—more students came from the top 1 percent of the income scale than from the entire bottom 60 percent."[12] Companies seeking to recruit a diverse workforce must deliberately look to schools that are most effective in enrolling students from low-income families.

An increasing number of U.S. citizens decline to identify themselves in narrow racial, socioeconomic, or cultural terms, and emphasize that they represent a mixture. The term, "intersectionality," now often used within the field of inclusion and diversity, underlines the fact that a person can experience interdependent, overlapping forms of discrimination based on categorizations such as race, gender, social class, or sexual orientation. This term was coined by Columbia University Professor Kimberle Crenshaw to explain how black women could experience prejudice both for being black and for being female.[13]

The banner of intersectionality has been raised by others to describe different kinds of hyphenated identities. Understanding that exclusion occurs in various ways which can impact a single individual surely helps to enable a more accurate and customized approach to analyzing problems and identifying solutions. This also opens up avenues for individual expression by people who may have been previously uncomfortable describing important aspects of their life experience (e.g., military service, immigrant status, religious beliefs, sexual orientation). In addition to black women, other groups face multi-faceted challenges that are perpetuated by institutionalized discrimination and political disenfranchisement.

Critics, on the other hand, particularly those with a socially conservative perspective, claim that the concept of intersectionality sometimes reinforces a heightened sense of victimhood and a new type of "us" versus "them" mentality—the person or group facing the most disadvantages is the most abused, long-suffering, and deserving of special treatment. Whether the outcome in any particular instance is progress toward greater inclusiveness or wrangling based on so-called identity politics likely depends upon the approach and attitudes of everyone involved: litigation or mutual outreach, ideology or dialogue, stereotypes or personal character, self-righteous protest or constructive change.

Multiculturalism is another U.S. trend that shares characteristics with intersectionality. It was most notably punctuated by the election of former President Obama, who was the son of a white mother from the state of Kansas and a black father from Kenya. An increasing number of citizens identify themselves as members of more than one race. There is a substantial literature on the subject of "third culture kids" that describes how children raised with multiple cultural identities—for example, through emigration or living part of their childhood abroad—can come to terms with their personal backgrounds.[14] Concepts such as "marginality" capture a common self-perception voiced by many with a multicultural background: "I don't really feel that I belong anywhere." Sadly, some never manage to turn this background into an advantage, living instead with a perpetual sense of being an outsider. Yet others leverage their multi-faceted cultural and linguistic fluency to achieve extraordinary levels of competence as business or government leaders, becoming serial bridge-builders between different worlds. Companies now frequently turn to multicultural individuals when establishing diverse teams or expanding subsidiaries abroad.

There is a substantial literature on the subject of "third culture kids" that describes children raised with multiple cultural identities.

> ### Inclusion in the U.S.: Implications
>
> *Inclusion efforts need to address deep-rooted issues such as interpersonal and institutionalized racism. They may also encounter resistance from employees, particularly those within the millennial workplace generation, who do not consider themselves to be members of a single racial, ethnic, or cultural group (including the millennial category), but want to be understood on their own terms. Others regard themselves as disadvantaged based on their economic background or other factors, even though they do not fall into any group that is legally defined as a "protected class." Process changes and program designs should take such perspectives into account; simultaneously, change leaders must be prepared to encounter pushback against "identity politics," disparaged by critics as fostering hypersensitivity and a sense of victimhood.*

Inclusion Initiatives: Questioning Basic Assumptions

Attention to regional and local variations around the world can lead to insights that require adjustments to inclusion initiatives. Social ideals, terminology, business processes, and communication styles taken for granted at headquarters are not necessarily shared by employees around the world who have been living in very different environments. **Efforts to establish common organizational goals, principles, and standards of conduct are often still feasible, however, if they are adapted based on local knowledge.**

For example, here are discoveries made by a Western facilitator during a leadership development program held in Kenya with participants from across sub-Saharan Africa who had been identified as high-potential future leaders. At first she found that her attempts to spark discussion did not seem to work.

> ### Leadership Development in Kenya
>
> *The initial atmosphere was one of suspicion and mutual distrust among the multinational hodgepodge of local employees and expatriates who made up the audience. There were too many inappropriate side remarks and put-downs, sighs and rolled eyeballs. The non-Africans in the group had received previous training of sorts at their past companies and in schools—they clearly had an advantage and were dominating the discussions while being subtly condescending toward, and ridiculing, the Africans. This did little for the willingness of participants to work and learn together.*
>
> *Everyone seemed to be distracted with the business of establishing a pecking order within their own subgroup. During the breaks they would form separate clusters divided by nationality and rank. There was an odd dynamic even among the Kenyans themselves—several appeared to be a bit aloof from the others, who deferred very cautiously to them. It turned out that three individuals who stood apart were members of elite and powerful family groups. The others not only treated them with respect, but appeared to be intimidated by them and went out of their way to avoid disagreement.*

Recognizing the divisive atmosphere in the room and evidence that some people were fearful about participating freely, the facilitator made adjustments to arrange for shorter days with everyone together in a large group format, creating separate time slots for one-on-one meetings with participants, plus more small-group discussion. These changes led to further insights and unexpected challenges to standard Western assumptions about inclusive leadership, particularly related to the constructive application of power:

- **Empowerment**

    A common line of skeptical questioning was directed at the description of management's role in delegating tasks and "empowering" employees to carry them out. Delegation was fine in the participants' view, but they would ask,

    Who is really going to give away power? If you trust such people, they may pretend to represent you and support you, but then they will misuse the information you provide them or turn against you to serve their own agenda. When you make a fine show of empowering others, then it is easier to blame them when things go wrong!

- **Terminology**

    The materials brought from headquarters were seen as having too much unhelpful jargon.

    This is the company's clever way of manipulating us. They try to tell us that this is a common global language, but it's one that only they can speak. They're not fooling anybody.

- **Strategic Planning**

    The program segment on strategic planning met with a deflating response from some participants that seemed to be a reflection of socioeconomic gaps and attitudes toward time.

    I'm just happy to be alive today. If you're a privileged person, you can think about planning. If you're not, you must deal with whatever God gives you.

- **Insiders and Outsiders**

    Participants struggled with the idea of inclusion, noting that one's inner circle, as they defined it, was of course treated in a very different way from how those on the outside were treated. However, when urged to reframe the way they saw themselves within the company and to add new and expanded groups of insiders, this was a challenge they took quite seriously and which visibly impacted ways in which group members related to one another.

With persistence and adjustment, key inclusion principles began to take hold. These were expressed in forms that were unexpected and yet strikingly effective, and inclusion began to take on its own distinctively local tone.

> ### Leadership Development in Kenya (continued)
>
> *At one point a senior participant launched into a story. The facilitator considered interrupting this person as he headed off into what appeared to be unrelated subject matter, but then noticed that the rest of the audience was riveted by the vibrancy, the rhythm, and the colorful punctuation of his tale. The man recalled the tough times the subsidiary had faced during an economic downturn—how their company had almost pulled out of the country due to political interference and the lack of profits. After several more minutes of recounting this history, the storyteller turned to the way that the foreign subsidiary president at the time had consulted with others from various backgrounds, testing several alternatives before deciding on the proper course of action. The story culminated with a perfect illustration of inclusive leadership as the listeners nodded and murmured their assent.*[15]

CHAPTER NINE

Inclusive Leadership Development

 *How can inclusive leadership be incorporated into leadership development programs?*

Global organizations' efforts at leadership development often lag behind the rapidly evolving business landscape. Many programs are still designed from a headquarters perspective and calibrated for a relatively narrow group of participants, neglecting markets and groups of employees critical to the company's future. Large-scale demographic trends and shifts in economic momentum have been gathering strength for decades. In addition, it is quite likely that leaders will have to respond to future events that are unanticipated and unprecedented.

> Leaders must constantly have their antennae up to anticipate and respond to inevitable change, and one vital way to do this is through fully embracing inclusivity.

Futurists warn that it is a mistake to assume that the years to come will unfold in a logical extension of present trends. Non-linear events have always shaped human affairs as well, and their magnitude along with the rate of change seems to be increasing. Geopolitical upheavals, natural disasters, the impact of disruptive technologies—we can predict that such events will occur, but with only limited specificity. Over the past twenty years, the world has experienced terrorist attacks, armed conflicts, and extreme weather events linked with global warming. Meanwhile, technologies have emerged that once seemed remote or implausible such as social media, smartphones, artificial intelligence, autonomous vehicles, and genetic modification.[1]

People in leadership roles will need to respond both to visible trend lines and to the unknowns that lie ahead. "The future is already here. It's just not very evenly distributed." This quote, sometimes attributed to the science fiction writer William Gibson,[2] suggests that we are surrounded by clues and incipient trends, but these are hard to ferret out and often frustratingly opaque. **Leaders must constantly have their antennae up to anticipate and respond to inevitable change, and one vital way to do this is through fully embracing inclusivity.**

Leadership Development: Fatal Flaws

So how is the practice of leadership development handling the massive tectonic shifts in demographics and global economic growth, or cultivating leaders who can respond flexibly to future events? Although leadership programs utilized by major multinationals typically incorporate a polite nod to the value of inclusion, many also share characteristics that can easily reinforce and perpetuate a dangerous corporate myopia. Here are a few common characteristics of both corporate leadership centers and renowned executive education programs that may lead participants to underestimate the significance and the challenges of key growth markets and demographic changes, as well as the need for more inclusive approaches.

Luxury Learning

People who design leadership development programs often have great affection for high-tech learning centers. The audio-visual equipment is sharp and reliable, there are comfortable accommodations nearby, travel arrangements are straightforward, it is feasible to invite top executives, and a location near headquarters provides access to strategy gurus and leading-edge R&D technology. A program held at this type of center is likely to be safe, predictable, and enjoyable for participants.

The problem with such venues is that they are almost completely unlike major emerging markets in which the organization must learn to win against aggressive competitors, nor do they reflect the conditions in slums and factory districts that often remain unseen across town in the same cities where employees live and work.

Our evolving world is messy and unpredictable. Some locations have a dynamism and speed of change that is difficult to grasp unless you witness it in person; others are mired in conflict and chaos, with disenfranchised citizens longing for change. Corporate learning centers provide a view from the top of the corporate mountain, but not a visceral sense of the gap between rich and poor, squalid living conditions, traffic congestion, power outages, corruption, youthful consumer preferences, or fast-moving new market forces. Statistics, trends, and case examples from distant lands seldom convey real vividness or urgency. Likewise, poverty and prejudice at home along with calls for social justice may seem distant even when they come from next door.

The Parade of Professors

Academic experts can provide deep insights and relevant special expertise, whether the topic is finance, marketing, strategy, or innovation. For leadership program organizers, there is also a level of security and reassurance in inviting an expert with an established reputation. However, the net result is seldom linked to a real "crucible" experience.

Professors accustomed to Western business school examples and learning styles tend to neglect the interests and potential contributions of non-Western or minority participants. Reward systems also matter, and these can affect the contributions of most professional educators. Faculty members at top universities are rewarded for prolific publishing in their areas of specialization, not for customizing learning solutions to meet an organization's specific needs or spending a lot of time getting to know program participants. They are often happy to fill a slot in a leadership program and pocket a nice paycheck, but then they want to get back to their own work. They are seldom inclined to expend extra effort in learning about the strategic priorities and unique business circumstances of their corporate clients (unless of course these serve their research purposes); nor are they motivated to collaborate with other program faculty by exchanging information, reinforcing common themes, and creating a seamless participant experience. The outcome can be a series of disconnected lectures that are informative but fail to draw out less strident voices or to have a transformational impact on participants.

Expert Executives

The concept of "leaders teaching leaders" has become a part of numerous leadership development programs, and was established as a regular practice in the latter part of the previous century at General Electric's Crotonville and other major corporate learning centers. Leadership program participants typically look forward to the chance to rub shoulders with top executives, and many executives themselves relish the chance to share their own stories and accumulated organizational wisdom.

A potential issue with such executive involvement is that it might reinforce concepts and methods from the slow-growth center of the enterprise while undervaluing opportunities in non-traditional markets. A "leaders teaching leaders" approach generally relies on headquarters-based leaders to do the teaching. Some of these executives are akin to generals who were victorious in a previous war and are still trying to apply the same tactics to the next one, even though the technology and the field of battle have altered radically. Leaders who have never actually lived in a high-growth market may have a cognitive understanding of the business, but are unable to provide relevant practical advice about how to lead effectively in places where logistical challenges, ambiguous market data, employee turnover, nimble local competitors, and government meddling are commonplace. They sometimes also assume that models and systems that have worked elsewhere can be readily imported, even when this is highly problematic.

Canned Culture

There is increasing recognition that culture—whether national or organizational—is a crucial factor in activities such as building effective virtual teams, integrating new acquisitions, or rolling out new organization-wide systems. Yet culture is usually an afterthought in leadership development programs. When it is introduced, culture is often presented in a "canned" format that presents country profiles, tidy distinctions, well-rehearsed stories about cross-border branding snafus, and hackneyed do's and don'ts, while neglecting to tie this to compelling business or mindset challenges.

The keenest irony in this form of "canned culture" presentation, and in leadership programs in general, is that is that the actual diversity

---
Culture is usually an afterthought in leadership development programs.
---

in the room may be underutilized or ignored. Leadership program participants from minority backgrounds or from other parts of the world are often quiet due to language differences, deference toward senior executives, a lack of confidence in the face of executive peers, or a reluctance to put forward personal viewpoints with which others may disagree. Given a real forum for expression, such participants would share their own valuable perceptions of employee engagement issues, local cultural variations and contradictions, and changes affecting consumer tastes and buyer preferences. They could demonstrate the relevance of cultural knowledge for dealing with unfamiliar environments at home and abroad, and for organization development. However, the culturally-embedded design of most leadership programs—which assumes, among other things, that participants will actively speak up, challenge, ask questions, and voice opinions with which others may disagree—normally ensures that executive participants most comfortable with the dominant culture play leading roles in discussions and team projects, while others hold back.

Unintended Consequences

In short, **existing leadership programs tend to reinforce mature market perspectives, while unintentionally blocking or trivializing diverse viewpoints**—especially from people or locations that could provide the greatest future growth opportunities and competitive threats. Program participants who have relevant experience are often marginalized and judged negatively based on their hesitation to jump in and express their views according to current executive standards for assertive discourse and polished presentation skills; sometimes these standards are even codified in the form of allegedly "global" leadership competencies. At their seductive worst, such programs can instill a sense of overconfidence in headquarters-based participants that they have mastered global leadership skills by going through an elite experience and hearing from relevant experts, when

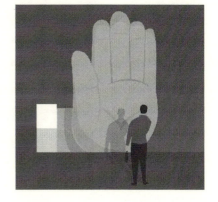

they instead have been insulated from voices that could perhaps better help them to face present and future market realities. Meanwhile, participants from other backgrounds may go away shaking their heads in disappointment at their own performance and with the disinclination of others to seek out their points of view, much less heed their advice.

How can leadership development break out of this damaging set of design flaws and the insular patterns of behavior that they support, particularly if the organization's long-term survival depends on success in unfamiliar environments?

The Crux of Leadership Development: Diversifying Experiences

An interesting line of recent psychological research focuses on so-called "diversifying experiences," which are defined as "unusual and unexpected events that... violate normality, break cognitive schemas, and promote a thinking style characterized by cognitive flexibility."[3] Such experiences are linked with the crucible experiences cited in Chapter 2, along with research on the correlation between overseas assignments and higher levels of creativity. Diversifying experiences, by transgressing the usual rules and boundaries that exist in our minds, stimulate individuals to examine challenges in a different way and to adopt new problem-solving strategies. The increased cognitive flexibility fostered through this mental adjustment process is described as "the ability to break old cognitive patterns, overcome

> **Diversifying experiences, by transgressing the usual rules and boundaries that exist in our minds, stimulate individuals to examine challenges in a different way and to adopt new problem-solving strategies.**

functional fixedness, and thus, make novel (creative) associations between concepts."[4]

This type of flexibility is essential not only for creativity, but also for effective leadership in a changing business environment. Studies of successful global leaders have produced similar terms—frame-shifting, agility, dexterity—that have become common features of the global leadership lexicon.[5] **Cognitive flexibility provides a missing link between multicultural environments and diverse domestic settings because the ability to step back from fixed mental patterns and to create new ones is essential for functioning effectively in both.** This appears to be closely associated with emotional flexibility in the form of heightened empathy and personal resilience as well.

Diversifying experiences that build cognitive and emotional flexibility are also vital for countering insular leadership development patterns. A particularly valuable finding of the research on this topic is that these experiences come in many forms, ranging from extreme to mild: early loss of a parent, living abroad, the experience of prejudice, or even perceived violations of the laws of physics. Profound life experiences such as personal tragedies or large-scale business crises cannot be readily timed or pre-planned, and expatriate assignments are time-consuming and expensive, but there are other learning opportunities that are more readily available.

For instance, exposure to the customs and ideas of immigrants, who are currently the topic of much controversy, may be a source of diversifying experiences, as there is a historical link between periods of increased immigration and exceptional creative achievement. Even virtual reality experiments have produced statistically significant results. One study found that subjects in a virtual reality environment who actively experienced unexpected events such as a suitcase on a table that increased or decreased in size depending on their proximity, or who were instructed to prepare a sandwich in an unorthodox way, scored higher than control group participants on subsequent measurements of cognitive flexibility.[6]

It still appears to be true that the more acute and long-lasting the experience of pattern-defying incongruity a person encounters, the more profound the developmental impact, affirming Nancy Adler's observation that the deeper the culture shock, the greater the learning.[7] Nevertheless, the evidence that relatively minor violations of what one previously thought to be common sense are also conducive to meaningful learning opens up a variety of fresh possibilities for leadership development; it becomes possible to consider a range of more or less structured experiences that can be leveraged for their developmental value. **Leadership crucibles, it turns out, come in contrasting sizes and with different temperature settings, and hold the potential for various kinds of learning.** Here is a list of possible experiences along with comments suggesting related assumptions that could be challenged.

Crucible Experiences: Warm to Hot

- Virtual reality game ("Physical objects are not moving the way they are supposed to.")

- Conversation with an immigrant work colleague ("I had no idea about what she went through to get here, the struggles she has experienced, or her impressions of me.")

- Attending an employee resource group meeting ("I thought that everyone in our company felt that they were treated equally.")

- Stretch goals ("We're not going to get there with the old methods. I'm going to have to find a new way.")

- Demanding boss ("What I had thought was a solid performance turned out to be mediocre in the eyes of my manager.")

- Action learning project ("People from other functions brought perspectives that were very different from mine.")

- Design thinking project ("Customers reacted very differently to our prototype model than we had anticipated.")

- Disruptive technology development ("This technology will change the basis of competition in our industry.")

- Leading a global team ("I learned that I need to do a lot more to draw out the opinions of all team members.")

- Assignment to a new function ("I am going to have to develop a new skill set to be successful in this role.")

- Expatriate assignment ("Most of my team members quit, and I was not going to meet my objectives; I had to hire new team members and find a different way to manage people in this country.")

- Encountering prejudice ("I thought that I was a valued member of this organization, but it seems I'm being regarded as a second class citizen with limited possibilities for getting ahead.")

- Crisis management ("This event wasn't supposed to happen and is not in my job description; I'm not prepared for such a huge, high stakes role.")

- Personal loss ("Losing a parent turned my whole world upside down.")

Leadership Program Design

Although the items listed above are very different, each entails a struggle with circumstances that were unanticipated and incongruous in comparison with the person's prior experience and assumptions, while offering the possibility for an active response. Leadership development programs can both create and tap into such experiences, and without this feature miss a precious opportunity for maximum impact.

Inclusion in its broadest form integrates people from diverse backgrounds—along with the ideas and information that they bring—to benefit employees, the organization, and customers. Two ways of creating diversifying experiences in the context of a formal leadership development program are to either take participants to new markets or to incorporate diverse perspectives at headquarters.

First-hand Experience

At least one segment of many executive leadership programs can be productively dedicated to direct, first-hand experience of fast-growth markets at home or abroad. While leaders may have seen numerous reports about countries such as India, China, Indonesia, or Nigeria, there is no substitute for going to a place to fully grasp its significance. Most of the world's growth markets are dynamic environments where thousands of citizens are entering the middle class each day, and millions move each year from the countryside to the city. These are incredibly rich learning environments where people new to such settings meet with surprises just walking down the street.

It is of course possible to go to a new location and spend a safe and comfortable week in hotel meeting rooms, with little outside contact. We recommend instead an intensively inclusive agenda that includes direct contact with:

- Local employees
- Expatriates
- Customers
- Competitors
- Suppliers

- Distributors
- Joint venture partners
- Government officials

Systematic daily debriefings and group discussions regarding each of these encounters help to surface outmoded assumptions and to consolidate new learnings. They also provoke wider questioning about risks and growth opportunities, unanticipated customer demands, disruptive forms of innovation that are occurring outside of a company's home market, new sources of competition, government initiatives, regulatory hurdles, and supply chain challenges.

Leadership program coordinators tend to shudder at all the things that can go wrong with schedules and logistics in emerging market environments. But this inherent messiness and unpredictability can be seen either as horrifying or as part of the learning experience. Delayed flights, power outages, choked traffic on bumpy, dusty roads, animals in the street, and motorcycles carrying families of six or seven all provide unforgettable messages about the nature of the local marketplace. Leaders from tidy developed countries also experience a vivid sense of their own limitations and/or potential for personal growth. Some revel in the market dynamism and opportunities, while others recoil at the sights, sounds, and smells—even the sheer press of humanity in crowded urban settings. Testing one's dietary limitations or willingness to try new foods offers non-trivial learnings about flexibility and resilience. "Agility," a term often bandied about in leadership programs, is not merely cognitive but also a gut-level response to witnessing urban poverty, experiencing the effects of polluted air and water, feeling violations of personal space, eating unfamiliar foods, and sweating or freezing in an unfamiliar climate.

Over the years, we have witnessed many "aha" moments from program participants that occurred on the spot. Each of the quotes below shows evidence of how diversifying experiences can stimulate fresh cognitive flexibility and non-habitual responses:

- *I have a new respect for one of our local competitors. I had thought they were a couple of product cycles behind us, but now I know that they are much closer to our level of quality, with a price point that is thirty percent lower.*

- *I sat through a virtual meeting with my local colleagues here late at night and watched how they were verbally run over by my team members back at headquarters. Now I am much more deliberate in inviting them into team meetings and ensuring that they have their say—they have begun to share important market insights.*

- *The workers in the factory here are so young! I can't believe the product quality is near the top of our global system with an average worker age of twenty-six!*

- *Our brand is positioned completely differently in this market in a way that allows us access to a different type of customer.*

- *The experience I have in a slow-growth market in Europe could be very useful to my colleagues here who have not yet had to live through a market slowdown.*

- *Our China operation can supply product to our markets in Africa at a competitive price point that we couldn't achieve elsewhere.*

- *We will need to bring more sourcing and production here to India in order to meet local pricing expectations.*

- *We have employees based in this region who could really benefit from a short-term assignment abroad—it would be a big motivator to them, a useful retention tool, and a way to help them interface more effectively with their global colleagues. I've already started to make arrangements for this to happen.*

> - *Our joint venture partners in this country are actually very different from each other, and it is a mistake to think of them in the same way. We have to deal with them differently based on their internal politics and government ties.*
>
> - *We are looking to this country as a key growth market, and yet we have only a handful of local executives at the top levels. We need to accelerate talent development here in a major way.*

Another rather miraculous outcome of leadership programs focused on first-hand experience in fast-growth markets is that participants who reside in these locations are suddenly front and center. A leader from India or China, for instance, who might have stayed quietly in the background during a program held at headquarters, deferring to more vocal participants, is suddenly an authority to whom all participants turn. Local leaders earn fresh recognition for their market knowledge, multilingual skills, customer and employee contacts, and business results. Expatriates, too, who may have long felt that their perspective was neglected and their many labors ignored, now find themselves frequently tapped for insights about their current home. **A geographical shift in program location tends to produce a comprehensive re-sorting among participants: levels of participation, prestige, and respect all shift toward a new orientation focused on requirements for growth in expanding markets**. This, too, can be a revelation and an exercise in cognitive and emotional flexibility for participants who now have a new perspective regarding their own level of knowledge and the contributions that others could make.

Headquarters-based Programs: Inside-Out to Outside-In

It is possible for leadership programs based at headquarters to bring the "outside in," both in terms of content and process, and to avoid viewing the world from an "inside-out" perspective that excludes and imposes ideas on others. Embedding inclusive perspectives and practices requires a comprehensive approach that, instead of treating "canned culture" as a tidy module replete with other people's examples, regards the entire program as an opportunity for live, real-time discovery and culture-building.

Executive Experts

In contrast to one of the common program flaws mentioned previously, expert executive speakers who describe their own diversifying experiences—how they had their assumptions about people or markets tested and in response developed new, more flexible leadership patterns—can validate the importance of such experiences and serve as a role model. When program participants know that a person above them in the hierarchy whom they respect and admire has struggled to become more inclusive, this gives them permission to open up and talk about their own difficulties and questions.

360 Feedback

Feedback comes in various forms, and there are myriad delivery instruments, some better than others. The key function that any instrument should serve is to make inclusive leadership a challenge that is personal rather than abstract. One of the most vital aspects of any assessment exercise is to know the gaps between self-perception and the perceptions of others: "I thought I was a pretty inclusive leader, but some of the people I'm working with sure don't seem to think so!" Participants also learn how they are or are not unique. It is usually a relief to discover that others are struggling with similar issues; at the same time, it is crucial for each leader to recognize their own unique characteristics and style, which enables them to balance authenticity with a willingness to experiment with new patterns of behavior.[8] "Openness to experience" is one of the so-called Big Five personality traits most often associated with success living abroad—leaders who have a realistic sense of their profile in this area may choose to leap into a larger or smaller crucible for their next assignment.

Program Content

Participants are more likely to build inclusive leadership skills if they are introduced to a few basic models, techniques, and examples. Leadership behaviors such as self-awareness, invite the unexpected, and frame-shifting provide the basis for inclusivity, as does the related three-step process for bridge-building (see Chapter 2). It is also important to understand how inclusion is defined, one's own current stage on the path to greater inclusivity, and what practical next steps are possible. Inclusive leadership examples and best practices should incorporate a diverse array of subject matter in terms of geography, functions, culture, race and ethnicity, etc., so that participants from various backgrounds will feel that the material speaks to them.

Context and frameworks must be tied quickly to participants' direct experiences, either from their own past or sometimes even what is happening among them on the spot. If prompted, nearly everyone will be able to recall a time when they caused or experienced exclusion themselves, and were forced to question basic assumptions. Providing them with a format to describe these events helps to reinforce and build on prior lessons, to learn from others, and to expand their leadership repertoire. Leaders learn most readily from their peers, and they often find it quite exciting to share their own experiences with others using a simple format such as:

- Here's what I assumed
- Here's what I experienced
- Here's what I learned to do differently

Program Process

Psychological safety is a feature not only of high-performing teams (see Chapter 4), but also of leadership development programs that are firing on all cylinders. The same outward manifestations—roughly equal air time, a willingness to take risks and offer up untested ideas, and a rapid pace of mutual learning—hold true as well. Program facilitators may need to use every technique they know in order to establish this kind of climate as quickly as possible: setting ground rules, asking well-targeted questions, drawing out some participants, requesting others to hold back, using small groups of various sizes, conducting pair exercises, providing structured opportunities to contribute, holding panel discussions, asking for alternative points of view, pushing back against one-sided opinions, and blending different modalities such as short presentations, experiential learning, games, debate, poetry, or humor.

The most powerful facilitation techniques bring attention to real-time interactions in the room—for instance, a previously silent participant who has just offered a valuable perspective based on another's invitation—yet must be used with caution because they can either take the discussion to a whole new level or shut it down if someone feels embarrassed or criticized. At its best, active facilitation of live interactions reveals the complexity behind cultural generalizations (e.g., "Germans are very direct"; "Japanese nod their heads even when they disagree"; "Hispanics are family-oriented") by cheerfully exploring possible explanations that may confirm, contradict, elaborate, or qualify standard wisdom. Participants may also bring with them charged emotional baggage based on polarizing views in their environment, and facilitators need to act in a deft, neutral way to turn this into a listening and learning opportunity rather than rhetorical combat.

In addition to keeping participants busy and challenged, leadership development should provide chances for reflection, both personal and strategic. Diversifying experiences are more readily digested and installed as lasting behavior patterns or traits when people are given structured opportunities to recall the event, to enrich it with greater detail, and to absorb it more fully, reinforcing new neural pathways in the process.[9] Diaries, guided reflection, and silence all make reflection easier, and serve to balance the contributions of extroverts and introverts—the latter may offer up startling insights once they've had time to think carefully about a topic.

Coaching

Coaching enables leaders to dig in and apply what they are learning. Skillful coaches build trust quickly and clarify objectives, meanwhile holding up a mirror that a leader may or may not be eager to see. They ask great questions, know when to push and when to hold back, work with coachees to build and explore options, and ask for realistic commitments—always circling back to see if these have been met. They are thoughtful, unselfish, honest, persistent, challenging, and sometimes irritating.

Another key role that a coach can play is to identify narratives that a leader offers, whether these are positive or self-defeating, and to question their accuracy and utility.[10] As a veteran psychologist was fond of noting, "If you observe carefully, you'll see that nine out of ten people walking down the street are talking to themselves."[11] Leaders are no exception to this regular internal story-telling activity, and deeply entrenched stories (some possibly inherited from parents or colleagues) may be the most tenacious obstacles to increased cognitive and emotional flexibility.

A leadership program participant could have a terrific new insight thanks to a diversifying experience, but that precious step toward a more inclusive mindset is soon erased by several laps around a familiar mental story track that confirms old biases and precludes new and more effective action. The shockingly low rate of retained learning and application from some programs is probably due as much to this narrative hamster wheel as to urgent job demands that absorb the energy of participants upon their return to work. Good coaches will break this news gently and suggest that we can do better.

Inclusive Story-telling

Mental flexibility is reinforced and expanded through narrative flexibility. When the previous story no longer fits, it is time for a different one. Just as a strong organizational culture that is no longer suited to a changing business environment becomes a critical weakness, outmoded story lines—silent or voiced—do not serve leaders well. Because current events are perceived through an aged and cracking lens, such stories instigate misinterpretations, cause unintentional exclusion by blinding the story-teller to facts that don't fit the story, and if voiced they make the leader look out of touch. When inaccurate narratives are shared among groups of executives at home or expatriates abroad, they foster cliquish conduct and "shoot the messenger" responses to those who dare to offer more accurate views, or "not invented here" rejections of employees with better ideas. Leaders who are not fully engaged with current realities or emerging possibilities may find that their employees, too, become disengaged.

Story-telling is usually taught in a leadership context as an instrument for more effective persuasion or for exerting wider influence—by touching people's heartstrings or appealing to their values, leaders are more likely to gain support and to win that big investment in their project. But fresh stories that feature genuine examples of inclusive leadership are perhaps even more valuable. Some cultures feature master story-tellers who have spent a lifetime learning their craft and are hard to imitate. By capturing a practical example of how a crucible experience led them to question their assumptions and to change, leaders can reinforce inclusive patterns in their own minds, within their team, and throughout the organization. Simple narratives have the advantage of being short and credible:

> What I assumed:
>
> *Angela was new to the team. At first I had her pegged as an average contributor with limited*

> *future potential because she struggled to get up to speed on the project. I had already started to exclude her from discussions of complex technical issues.*
>
> What I experienced:
>
> *I misjudged her potential because she had come from a totally different line of business and was new to the company. When I started working with her more closely, I realized that she is incredibly bright and committed, and she responded to my feedback by learning quickly and volunteering to take on more responsibility. Now, after a year of working together, she is going to step into my role as team leader when I move to the next job. I never would have imagined this at first. Was I ever wrong about her!*
>
> What I learned:
>
> *From working with Angela I've learned to postpone judgment a bit, to work with team members more closely to figure out what their background is and what they are capable of doing, and then to start raising the bar while offering additional coaching to those who want it. This is what I'm doing with everyone on my new team, and it seems to be working.*

Everyday Inclusion

Leadership development programs provide useful ideas and tools along with an impetus to change. But they are also just one aspect of a growth process that spans a whole career, and are part of a much larger inclusion challenge. Organizations have an imperative and an opportunity to build inclusion at every level, taking a comprehensive approach to each phase of the global talent cycle.

At the same time, inclusion is ultimately a personal responsibility. It is up to each leader to assess where they are on their own inclusion journey and to consider the value to themselves, to others, and to the business of taking further steps. The vital next step that any leader can take is to identify and engage in everyday acts of inclusion that widen the circle of "us," while cultivating crucible experiences that will further expand minds and hearts.

CHAPTER TEN

Five Organizational Levers

 **What kinds of organizational changes are most essential to support inclusion? Is it possible to measure progress toward a more inclusive work environment?**

Inclusive actions flourish most readily in a supportive environment. Many leaders want to increase inclusion organization-wide, but are uncertain about where to start or what changes to prioritize in order to achieve their goals. A comprehensive approach to the inclusive leadership journey usually produces the best results, with special focus on five key levers of organizational support:

> Organizations need to be able to change and grow, to reinvent themselves in the face of shifting circumstances.

1. Recruitment
2. Executive Engagement
3. Coaching/Mentoring/Sponsorship
4. Key Performance Indicators
5. Policy and Process

This chapter combines our own experience with a sampling of recent research. Although many of the studies in this area are U.S.-centric, findings based on broader samples and international data are referenced where feasible, along with data from our own *Inclusive Behaviors Inventory*.

Lever #1: Recruitment

Competing successfully for talent means hiring the most capable recruits to grow markets and serve customers wherever a company has operations. In sought-after fields such as engineering or computer science, mid-career hires come at a premium price, and college students may have multiple internships under their belts and job offers in hand well before they graduate. What makes one firm's recruitment efforts more effective than another's?

Shifting technologies and global demographics mean that new employees are often different from their predecessors in many ways: technical training, native language, nationality, racial and ethnic background, communication styles, and so on. A core dilemma that most recruitment efforts face is *"How can we ensure a 'cultural fit' with our new recruits while opening our organizational culture to change at the same time?"* This dilemma overlaps with a common challenge that most leaders face when they are elevated to new and more complex roles: "What got you here won't get you there."[1] In other words, the very work patterns that have been the foundation for success thus far, either for an individual or for an organization, may become obstacles as the environment changes. Industries rarely stand still, and there is a constant imperative to preserve essential cultural elements and competencies that continue to be relevant—values, expertise, relationships—while injecting new ideas, perspectives, and energy.

Managers in charge of recruitment in larger organizations usually have a keen awareness of this dilemma, yet they are under pressure to meet targets and fill open job slots. Moreover, they must work with an extended network of employees who conduct job interviews or travel to job fairs and college campuses. This network sometimes includes people who are happy to return to their *alma mater*, to revitalize their prior connections, and to seek out others who fit with their own implicit success criteria. These key players in the recruiting process, however, may not be deliberately seeking to identify others who could be successful but are unlike them.

How can managers ensure that their entire extended team is working in an inclusive way? Here are some characteristics of successful recruiting teams:

Characteristics of Successful Recruiting Teams

- The entire recruiting team shares **common goals** for finding candidates who are both well-qualified and diverse, with special attention to areas in which the company needs to expand its representation in order to grow and serve the communities where it operates.

- **Job descriptions** are scrutinized for language that might cause qualified candidates to exclude themselves based on gender, race, or other characteristics (see Figure 10.1).

- Use **non-traditional methods** such as Boolean search (a method of using key words and modifiers to search, for example, for particular types of colleges, associations, or names) to locate underrepresented candidates and create a more diverse hiring pool.

- Interviewers use a **common set of questions** and a common process for recording responses and impressions to reduce the effects of subjectivity.

- Recruiting teams incorporate a **diverse set of perspectives** through steps such as two-person interview teams for high-priority candidates, with interviewers comparing their impressions afterward. (This does not necessarily mean that members of every interview team must fully reflect the diversity of the candidates under consideration, which may be unfeasible for some organizations and exhausting for underrepresented minority members.)

- Teams consider establishing a **minimum number of minority candidates to interview** to ensure that they start with a sufficiently broad candidate pool. It is best to have multiple candidates rather than just one.[3]

- Recruitment team members volunteer to take on different roles such as contrarian or **devil's advocate** to ensure that various viewpoints are considered. ("How much of a change agent will this person be? Is there another candidate who would challenge us more?")

- Teams consider establishing a **"blind audit" qualification process** focused on task performance, analogous to the practice of blind orchestra audits which has resulted in the selection of more female orchestra members than in the past. (See Figure 10.2.)

- Recruiting team members build the skills needed to **recognize and counteract unconscious bias** in interviews and selection. For example, each aspect of unconscious bias outlined in Chapter 3 can apply to the recruiting process. Here are simple examples using the CIAO model:

    Confirmation Bias: This candidate is like me, and therefore is more likely to be successful in my company than other candidates.

    Insider Bias: This recruit participated in many of the same groups and activities that I did during my university years, so I am confident that he will fit in well.

    Attribution Bias: Candidate A did well based on hard work and persistence; Candidate B received special treatment.

    Overconfidence: I know what my company needs and which qualifications are most essential for a successful career here.

Figure 10.1: Modifying Job Descriptions[2]

- Created software to provide clients feedback on the likelihood that a job description will attract diverse candidates.
- Looks for patterns in data related to job descriptions in postings (how many applied, how long the job was posted, the demographic groups it attracted).
- The tool highlights words based on how well they do or do not work to attract a diverse audience.
- Mozilla reports the software has helped them fill positions 17% more quickly.

Kieran Snyder
Cofounder and CEO, Textio

Cultural competence is relevant to recruiting team member preparation as well. Knowledge of culture-based behavior patterns can be important not only for dealing with international candidates, but also for making accurate judgments about diverse styles of work and communication within the same country. **"Intuition" is often misleading in an environment where people are assessing cues based on different cultural styles and behavior.**

For instance, an interviewer who is a very "Direct" communicator may underestimate candidates whose "Indirect" style leads them to be modest about prior achievements. Likewise, an "Independent," "Task-focused" interviewer may be put off by a candidate who gives a more "Interdependent" or "Relationship-oriented" response, even when that candidate has a strong track record of achievements. All team members should be prepared to recognize instances in which their own cultural profiles could cause them to misjudge candidates who are otherwise well-qualified and could be successful within their organization.

Figure 10.2: Blind Audition Process[4]

- Created an online blind-audition process where potential applicants are given a job to complete (e.g. web developers are asked to create a webpage). Hiring managers assess the completed task without any personal identifiers, including name, gender, work experience or educational background.
- Clients have seen a 60% jump in applicants from underrepresented groups compared to traditional screening.
- Reduces time to fill a position by almost 40%.

Kedar Iyer
Cofounder and CEO,
GapJumpers

Lever #2: Executive Engagement

Nearly every set of criteria for an organization-wide inclusion initiative underlines the importance of getting key executives on board. There are countless pitfalls when executives are not committed or are half-hearted supporters. Initiatives that begin with fanfare sputter out due to sporadic investment of time or money; decisions are made that ironically neglect the input of true inclusion champions; and employees observe that the actions of executives themselves are undermining basic inclusion principles. In the absence of sustained executive commitment, other priorities ultimately take precedence and the focus on inclusion fades, leaving a deep layer of skepticism throughout the employee population. On the positive side, there is increasing empirical evidence that support for diversity on the part of top management is linked with favorable business outcomes such as higher revenue from innovation.[5]

Executives are under relentless pressure to perform. These leaders need to hit their growth targets, limit expenses in the face of rising costs, keep customers happy, retain vital employees, and invest in the next generation of technology. They are normally pleased to be able to celebrate success, to raise compensation, and to hire more people; yet even in the midst of good times they have to keep the potential for harder days in their minds as well. In organizational life there are few things more painful than having to lay off employees when the market turns downward or, worse yet, to declare bankruptcy when expenditures exceed revenue and the banks refuse to extend further credit. Executive roles are normally quite visible, and failure could permanently damage reputations that have been built up over years of hard work.

Executives are naturally most responsive to initiatives that are tied to growth, cost optimization, or acquiring superior talent. They want to win, and have also been trained to probe investment proposals for strengths and weaknesses. "How exactly is your initiative going to help us?" they are likely to ask. There is no substitute for a rational, company-specific business case that ties a proposal, for example, to organizational goals for expansion in a promising market, reduced legal costs related to alleged discrimination, or being able to lure key talent away from rivals. If an objective is to hire and retain high-potential employees from all backgrounds, they will want to track progress and revisit this at regular intervals, just like their other goals.

Senior leaders who are most dedicated to inclusion also tend to have some prior experience that made it significant and personally poignant for them: a difficult stint living abroad; a family member with a disability; a relative who was sexually assaulted; a spouse who is an immigrant; a close friend who is a minority group member; or a personal brush with illness or death. Parenthood has an impact as well: "Research on male CEOs, politicians, and judges shows that fathers of daughters care more about gender equality than men without children or with only sons."[6] Those without such a background can still deepen their insight and commitment through the kinds of diversifying experiences described in Chapter 9 with 360 degree feedback that invites them to consider how they are perceived by the people around them, or possibly via corporate training efforts featuring exercises such as personal "story-telling" that help them to see into others' lives. Such events need to be facilitated with sensitivity to ensure that the result is insight and inspiration rather than perceived blaming and shaming.

Personal Histories

At an offsite retreat, executive team members were asked to describe aspects of their personal history others might not know about. Several of the stories that emerged were surprising to everyone. One leader, whom everyone assumed had come from

> *a wealthy family setting, described his childhood being raised on a farm, the scholarship that was his only chance to attend college, and the opportunity a former manager who believed in his potential had given him to move into a challenging new role that was a career game-changer.*
>
> *Another participant, who was one of the last to speak, said quietly that she was the only person from her small town in China to have passed the entrance exam for a university in Beijing and to have attended business school abroad, and that she was now sponsoring a program to enhance educational opportunities for girls back in her home province. The team members came away from the event with a much deeper appreciation for each other, and one summed up the shared spirit that emerged from their conversation by saying, "I'm going to help you in every way that I can, and I am committed to supporting every single one of our future leaders regardless of what their backgrounds are."*

There are potential downsides to executive enthusiasm, too. These include the large-scale, one-size-fits-all solution. Some corporate directors of inclusion and diversity have found themselves coping with sudden directives from leaders who have become true believers: "Women clearly face problems everywhere in the world. I've seen this with my own eyes. You have one goal this year, which is to raise the number of women managers company-wide!" Such directives may or may not constitute a reasonable next step, and they are sometimes not based on a broad and balanced inclusion strategy.

Another issue can be translating a single executive's enthusiasm to the rest of the leadership team and to mid-level managers who haven't yet caught fire in the same way. **Given the competitive and peer-conscious nature of people who have climbed the career ladder, a way to**

invite commitment is to establish project teams with specific goals: sell products to members of a growing minority population; preserve vital talent from a recent acquisition; build a more diverse pipeline of future leaders. Working together and even competing to make the biggest contribution on behalf of a common cause is frequently a more compelling invitation for senior leaders to get on board than is mandatory training.

Engaged executives normally also want to go beyond projects and task forces, and will look for a way to institutionalize inclusion efforts. Potential structures for sustaining inclusion over time include appointing a direct report to the CEO with a title such as Chief Diversity Officer (CDO), adding inclusion to the portfolio of the human resources department, or making this a responsibility of business units or divisions. There are potential pros and cons with each approach, and as a result many organizations create their own hybrid structures.

Chief Diversity Officer

Pros: This structure brings visibility to the topic of inclusion and diversity, and creates a clear line of accountability. It brings the CDO to the table with other members of the executive team, reinforcing their awareness of inclusion priorities.

Cons: Especially when there is little actual budget and few direct reports to this position, it can become more of a "movie star" role that enables line managers to avoid taking responsibility themselves. (One veteran of this role referred to it as having "alligator arms"—in other words, a short reach for actually getting things done.)

Human Resources

Pros: The human resources (HR) function has the personnel, both at headquarters and embedded within business units and regions, to follow through on initiatives. HR professionals can also ensure that inclusion initiatives are aligned and integrated with other policies and processes related to talent development, succession planning, and so on.

Cons: HR often has a long list of objectives, and a new addition to this list might be regarded as a low priority in the absence of explicit directives and a dedicated budget. The link with HR could imply ties with legal compliance measures in some organizations. Inclusion may not be seen as a business imperative by other departments; it will be associated with the image of the HR department, whether positive or negative.

Business Lines

Pros: When line managers take responsibility for inclusion, there can be considerable grass roots interest and energy, with specific applications to each part of the business. Many employees look to business leaders as role models, and real commitment by line managers transmits a clear message: "We are serious about this!"

Cons: If line manager adoption is uneven and uncoordinated, there are likely to be mixed signals and mixed results. Different managers may adopt their own homemade models and approaches, and, if this is the case, it will become difficult to track progress or disseminate best practices in a coordinated fashion.

Lever #3: Coaching, Mentoring, & Sponsorship

Research suggests that providing focused support to employees with backgrounds different from the organizational mainstream has a strongly positive effect on the advancement of minority employees.[7] This support can take a variety of forms, depending on career stage and corporate culture.

Coaching

New recruits from backgrounds outside of the corporate mainstream often find themselves a step or two behind from their first day in the organization. While others seem to dress appropriately, know the right things to say, and are off and running quickly, it may take longer for minority employees to learn their way around. The initial culture shock for them is greater, and they also frequently encounter subtle or not so subtle messages indicating that less is expected of them, or that they are expected to perform in a niche role with limited upside prospects. As a result, compared to members of the majority culture, it is common for this population to experience lower job satisfaction, negative performance evaluations, and higher attrition.

Coaching that is targeted at individuals or groups of early career employees can be useful in countering trends that over time tend to transform a diverse recruiting class into a homogeneous set of leaders. Although coaches are usually not positioned to call for organizational change, in their one-on-one conversations they can shed objective light on the internal narratives of employees that sometimes lead to conclusions such as, "My opportunities are limited," or "I just don't belong here." Women and minority employees in particular may have questions, beliefs, or doubts about themselves that foster a lack of self-confidence or willingness to take on risks for the sake of career advancement.

The examples in Figure 10.3 were gathered from a large pool of Asian women managers who attended a recent conference in Singapore, and reflect, in part, social expectations in the region that still place the main responsibility for family care and child-rearing on women while regarding men as the primary breadwinners.

Figure 10.3: Self-Limiting Questions & Beliefs: Examples

Coaching provides individuals with the chance to identify and test their own beliefs, while exploring which of those beliefs are based on real obstacles and which are unfounded. When this type of coaching is conducted in a small group context, it also allows participants to share their fears and concerns with each other and to learn that they are not alone in having doubts about their ability to succeed. Coachees are able to discuss possible solutions together and build a network of supportive contacts in the process. As self-limiting obstacles are addressed, coaching conversations can move on to identifying key areas for knowledge acquisition and skill-building, as well as discussing how to move forward with professional and personal development while addressing real obstacles.

Mentoring and Sponsorship

For employees who are candidates for management roles, mentors or sponsors serve several purposes. First, they can offer information, contacts, visibility, and candid feedback that candidates would otherwise miss out on, limiting their career opportunities and areas for professional growth. Choice leadership assignments are normally offered to insiders with whom top executives are already comfortable, and **effective mentors or sponsors help promising candidates step over the threshold from outsider to insider**.

Second, mentors or sponsors may provide encouragement and support for taking on responsibilities that candidates are capable of handling but hesitate to assume. Extensive interviews with women in one large organization produced a troubling set of findings for those committed to equal developmental opportunities. Many women observed that men are considered for, and accept, a role or promotion where they may not have all the qualifications or experience required. The trend for women, however, is that they are not considered for, nor will they accept, a role for which they do not feel completely qualified.

Other research suggests that a lack of confidence or hesitancy to take risks, both of which are sometimes attributed to gender differences, could actually be natural responses to organizational realities: "Because women operate under a higher-resolution microscope

than their male counterparts do, their mistakes and failures are scrutinized more carefully and punished more severely. People who are scrutinized more carefully will, in turn, be less likely to speak up in meetings, particularly if they feel no one has their back. However, when women fail to speak up, it is commonly assumed that they lack confidence in their ideas."[8] A gentle push—"You can do this!"—plus the knowledge that one has a supporter who is willing to provide both guidance and a safety net in case things go wrong, could be just enough for women or minority candidates to contribute more innovative ideas or to accept a challenging role they would otherwise decline. **An employee's image of what a different course of action or a new role entails could be getting in the way**, when in fact there are ways to prepare for or to avert potential problems.

Sponsors typically have the mandate to ensure that their protégé stays with the organization and is able to advance. Along the way, many become personally invested in their candidate's progress. Personnel decisions about recruiting or next-level positions tend to fall into a gray zone where biases easily take hold; under these kinds of circumstances minorities and women are more frequently evaluated critically and eliminated from the candidate pool, while men from the majority culture are given the benefit of the doubt.[9] Such decisions can be swayed by a credible advocate who is able to make a pitch on a candidate's behalf, both highlighting objective qualifications and conveying an emotional undertone of personal conviction. **A powerful and enthusiastic sponsor may go beyond encouragement and advocacy to take on the role of a "snowplow"** who helps to smooth the way for protégés, assuring that they will have opportunities commensurate with their abilities and be judged fairly for their performance. Some companies prefer to avoid putting an official

---

A powerful and enthusiastic sponsor may go beyond encouragement and advocacy to take on the role of a "snowplow"...

---

sponsorship program in place—appointing only mentors instead—because this might be seen as a form of favoritism toward certain employees; other firms are sufficiently alarmed by lower retention or promotion rates for targeted groups that they regard sponsorship as an indispensable method for leveling the playing field.

The utility of mentors and sponsors is clear, and benefits accrue to them as well as to the candidates they are supporting. Each individual who takes on such a role should keep in mind potential pitfalls.

Common Pitfalls for Mentors or Sponsors

- Rushing to be "helpful" without thoroughly understanding a protégé's circumstances, and providing guidance that fits the mentor's own experience and background but not those of the mentee

- Letting bias or stereotypes—e.g., "Women lack confidence," or "Minority candidates have advanced through affirmative action"—get in the way of a clear assessment of individual capabilities

- Trying to solve problems without sufficiently enabling mentees to figure things out and take action themselves where needed

- Letting mentees' self-doubts prevent them from taking on roles that they could handle

- Pushing protégés too hard to jump into roles they are not ready for; failing to understand what they can or cannot change in their own social context

- Failing to provide ongoing support to those who have taken on new challenges but are now struggling

- Allowing enthusiasm for their protégés and sense of competition with other sponsors lead them to create a new set of unfair advantages or disadvantages

Lever #4: Key Performance Indicators

The metrics used to gauge progress in inclusion tend to be relatively blunt instruments. It is easy to measure numbers of women, minorities, or people of various nationalities in management roles, for example, and there is of course value in establishing a baseline for comparison with external benchmarks and for setting future targets. What an organization chooses to prioritize and track will of course depend on the legal framework that governs its headquarters operations, the locations in which it has a presence, its business priorities and plans for growth, and its corporate mission and values.[10]

Several cautionary notes apply to the use of inclusion metrics, however. The first is that the mere presence of a diverse range of employees in different roles or at various levels does not guarantee positive business outcomes. Moreover, although for statistical purposes it is preferable to have clear and straightforward ways of categorizing people, the reality is usually more complex: "No one is just female, or just black, or just Muslim. Each person is 'a whole package of interlocking attributes.'"[11] Employees with multicultural backgrounds may also be reluctant to identify with any single nationality—this would force them to choose between parents, or between their current homes and their countries of origin. LGBTQ employees in some countries may push for non-binary gender categories, while in other places these categories are illegal. Racial classifications such as "white," "black," or "Asian" may fail to take into account differences in educational opportunities or socioeconomic backgrounds.

There is also research pointing to the value of "deep-level diversity"[12]—personality, values, and abilities—that is not immediately apparent or easy to track. Differences in cognitive styles fall into this category of less readily visible features as well. The leadership team attributes most closely linked to innovation, according to one recent study, are diversity in career path, industry background, national origin, and gender.[13] At the same time, employees who belong to racial minorities may feel that excessive focus on personalities or cognitive styles fosters neglect of the difficult work of addressing social inequities with deep historical roots, unequal distribution of power and privilege, and limited opportunities for advancement.

The presence of employees who straddle multiple categories can be regarded either as an obstacle or as a source of opportunities for deeper and more fine-tuned analysis. Organizations with data for large numbers of employees could be asking questions that might lead to effective follow-up measures:

- Is there a difference in the functional backgrounds of women who advance in our organization versus those who do not?

- Are some nationalities more successful than others?

- Are Hispanics with an international background promoted at the same rate as those with a domestic background?

- When individuals join as mid-career hires from similar or different industry backgrounds, how do they progress in comparison with other employees?

Follow the Talent Cycle

The diversity of executive teams or board members receives considerable attention due to media scrutiny, but the entire talent cycle merits careful examination. To track the progress of a particular group or groups of people over time—most commonly based on gender, race, or nationality—it is valuable to establish measurements for each phase of the employee life cycle. Leaders confronted with a lack of diversity in their ranks are tempted to say, "The main problem is our recruitment pipeline. We have to hire more qualified recruits to increase our pool of talent!" This helps to kick the can down the road while avoiding the need for close scrutiny of day-to-day organizational patterns, especially when ownership for metrics is delegated to a staff function such as the chief diversity officer or human resources rather than being owned by each line of business. However, the value of inclusive practices comes from their application to the full path from fresh recruit to executive, and from holding line management as well as staff functions accountable. See Figure 10.4 for common metrics that can be applied to successive stages of the employee talent cycle.

Figure 10.4: Talent Cycle Metrics[14]

- ***Recruitment***: Is the company hiring qualified employees from select institutions or industry backgrounds in the targeted categories?

- ***Representation***: Does the demographic profile of employees reflect the general population and/or the available pool of technical specialists?

- ***Workplace Climate***: How do the satisfaction rates for different groups of employees compare with each other based on race, gender, age, rank, or nationality?

- ***Compensation***: Are employees in the same job categories being paid at equal rates regardless of their background?

- ***Retention***: Is the organization successful in retaining employees of all categories at the same rate, and if not, which groups tend to have higher or lower rates of attrition?

- ***Promotion***: Are all groups promoted at the same rate at each level of advancement? If not, which groups tend to move ahead or fall behind, and at what point in their careers?

- ***Succession***: Is there a robust, diverse pipeline of future executives with the right experience to step into top jobs?

Other metrics that some firms examine include participation in skill-building programs as well as costs related to prevention, investigation, and legal defense of employee discrimination claims. On an optimistic note, some organizations have targeted specific initiatives based on skill requirements and a sense of social mission. SAP, for instance, is in the midst of a multi-year recruiting and onboarding effort that will increase the number of "neurodiverse" employees to 1% of its total workforce—a number chosen because it corresponds roughly to the percentage of people in the general population with a diagnosis of autism.[15] And for companies with international operations, tracking whether they have sufficient local national talent with the requisite skills to drive future plans for growth and market penetration becomes another vital metric.

Measuring Inclusive Actions

The five dimensions that comprise the *Inclusive Behaviors Inventory* provide a model for building individual self-awareness and commitment to inclusive actions. This framework can also be useful for measuring inclusion on the organizational level in order to identify and address common challenges.[16]

Combined survey results from a variety of companies and industries indicate that, among the five dimensions discussed throughout this book, "Working Across Boundaries" is the area in which respondent self-ratings are the lowest across the board.[17] Such evidence is not surprising, as even people who are comfortable working with certain aspects of diversity—say, working across organizational functions—are still quite likely to identify other areas—for instance, racial

Figure 10.5: Inclusive Behaviors Inventory

Learning about Bias | Building Key Skills | Working Across Boundaries | Becoming a Champion | Getting Results

or generational differences—with which they are relatively uncomfortable. Two of the lowest scoring items within this "Working Across Borders" survey dimension single out differences in gender and cognitive styles. For an organization that mirrors such overall results, targeting selected development opportunities related to this particular survey dimension or items within it could be components of an effective strategy.

Lever #5: Policy & Process

Experience with well-meaning initiatives to foster greater inclusion has demonstrated that some methods work better than others. Ineffective methods can even have unintended negative consequences. For example, mandatory diversity training may produce a backlash among employees who continue to discriminate in subtle ways; testing designed to promote fairness is sometimes applied unfairly to screen out minorities but not others; and grievance systems tend to spark retaliation. Each of these methods is actually correlated with declines in the number of women and minorities in management roles.

Meanwhile, alternative methods such as voluntary training, mentoring, task forces, and dedicated diversity managers are correlated with relatively positive outcomes.[18] Other research points to the need for a foundation of inclusive organizational practices that appears to be necessary in order to reap the potential benefits of diversity; these include participative leadership, equal pay for equal work, and a strategic emphasis on diversity and inclusion led by the CEO.[19]

Psychological Leverage

Such positive or negative results appear to be influenced by basic psychological principles, including aspects of unconscious bias that were presented in Chapter 3. Humans value the capacity for autonomous action—which is linked with one's basic sense of control over environmental circumstances and ability to handle stress—and tend to react negatively when their autonomy is threatened by directives issued without consultation.[20] "Insider" versus "outsider" dynamics shape whether a candidate for employment or promotion is subjected to rigorous testing. Having a grievance filed against you or your department could produce an instinctive "fight" response, possibly due in part to overconfidence that your own department is blameless. In addition, a form of confirmation bias known as anchoring influences managers who read employee self-evaluations before writing their assessments, leading them to unintentionally reward self-promotion and punish modesty.[21]

Those who shape policies and processes designed to promote inclusion are well advised to not only take these aspects of the human psyche into account, but to turn them to their advantage. **Voluntary training or task force participation enables participants to preserve their own sense of autonomy while shaping an updated concept of themselves as supporters or champions of inclusion.** Structured recruiting interviews and involvement of minority team members can counter insider bias and produce a sense of teamwork in service of a common cause. Leaders who convincingly describe their own inclusion journey, perhaps through transformative personal experiences or encounters with workplace colleagues, encourage employees to drop their "fight" response to perceived threats, responding instead with empathy. And when managers view employee self-assessments after they have formulated their own evaluations rather than before, this enables them to judge more objectively and to better coach those with inflated self-images as well as those who lack confidence.[22]

Informal organizational practices may be more powerful and pervasive than formal ones, and are reinforced by social values that shape role expectations. Analysis of how office "housework" assignments—taking notes, handling meeting logistics, ordering food, planning parties, keeping lists of tasks, and so on—are made in comparison with the process for assigning coveted growth opportunities indicates that the less prestigious roles are assigned disproportionately to women and minorities, including employees hired for professional roles.[23] Similarly, many organizations send informal signals through office space allocations, forms of recognition, or even pictures displayed on the walls. **It is worth examining these kinds of informal aspects of office life for the signals they send about fairness and equal access to opportunities.** Seemingly small adjustments can have a surprisingly large symbolic effect. Work-life flexibility is another area where both informal and formal policies come into play. Although organizations normally have formal policies related to childbirth, for example, actual practices vary widely according to national laws, health issues, family situation, and individual preferences. Conducting a personalized check-in with each individual before, during, and after maternity or paternity leave helps employees to feel that they are valued and will be able to continue their careers in ways that fit their own aspirations; adopting a child holds its own distinctive set of challenges for which employees may need understanding and support.[24]

Policy & Process Overview

- Executive sponsorship and role modeling
- Participative leadership practices
- Task force participation
- Voluntary training
- Structured recruiting interviews
- Equal pay for equal work
- Coaching and mentoring
- Peer group support; prevention of "onliness"
- Performance assessment prior to viewing self-evaluations
- Fair distribution of office housework; development opportunities
- Informal signals: office space; recognition; pictures on the wall
- Work-life flexibility
- Dedicated inclusion and diversity function

Career Crossroads

Beyond formal and informal measures to increase organization-wide inclusion, intensive efforts targeted at specific career points are also very useful. Our experience with a variety of organizations in different industries suggests that there are three particularly crucial inflection points, or career crossroads:

> **A. Onboarding:** If the starting point for a career is compared with a marathon run, not everyone is toeing the same starting line on the first day of work. Some are suited up and ready to go, having practiced for years and ready to take off at a sprint, eyeing fellow racers who are equally well-prepared. Others are still getting dressed for the race, wondering what a marathon is, or are delayed on the subway trying to get to the starting point. If you are the first person in your family to have a professional career, are self-conscious about how you stand out as a racial minority, are working in a white collar workplace environment for the first time, and/or are unsure that your prior education and training have prepared you adequately for this new job, you are likely to start out at a different pace.
>
> A structured onboarding program for all employees addresses this unequal starting point issue in several ways. It provides everyone with a shared basis of knowledge about the organization, a common introduction to organizational values and strategy, and insider tips that may otherwise filter through to some new employees but not to others. Such onboarding can also include teambuilding exercises that encourage a sense of camaraderie, self-awareness, shared purpose, and mutual inquiry rather than rivalry and unexamined bias.
>
> **B. First Promotion:** The KPIs favored by many organizations regularly provide findings that are both startling and disappointing. **In spite of extensive**

recruiting efforts targeting women and minorities, for example, such groups often fall behind the overall performance curve in their early career stages, receiving low assessments on average and thus fewer chances for advancement. This marked difference in performance ratings usually begins with the first assessment and extends through initial promotion decisions at the two- to five-year mark (depending on the industry). Employees who see themselves already falling behind their peers at this stage are less likely to be fully engaged at work or to sign up for the next stage of training or testing. They are also more likely to leave, and the organization's talent pipeline suddenly begins to sprout leaks.

Rather than blaming recruiters for not finding the right talent and then repeating this pattern with another crop of new hires, it is better to apply more systemic solutions to the causal factors that appear most salient. Targeted internship programs prior to full-time employment, for instance, are commonly linked with better performance results for minority hires than for those without an internship experience—this makes sense because employees who have been interns take on full-time jobs with a good understanding of the corporate culture and a fairly clear sense of performance expectations. Additional measures that can prevent women and minorities from falling behind and curb attrition include foundational onboarding for all employees and coaching for select individuals or groups, as discussed previously. These steps help to address the issue that some recruits arrive better prepared than others, and that qualified individuals may be holding themselves back through self-limiting beliefs or the sense that they are not a good fit for the workplace.

A related area of research focuses on the positive effect of having more than one woman or minority member on a team, rather than just one such individual who generally experiences greater isolation and more biased interactions.

> *Whether on executive teams or within an everyday workplace context, the implication is that it is better to assign two or more employees in one location rather than to spread women or minorities so thin that they all experience the negative effects of "onliness."*[25]

Peer relationships created through group coaching are another way to build a network among individuals who might otherwise feel isolated.

The first-line manager or supervisor also plays a critical role. It is most effective to apply a three-legged stool of support for employees facing a crucial career inflection point that is linked with frequent, unwanted turnover. Two of the three legs are coaching that promotes self-reflection and resilience, and a mentor/sponsor who offers insider insights, encouragement, and opportunities or a more responsible role when this is warranted. **The third, most often neglected leg of the stool, is the direct manager or supervisor**. Research has long identified the relationship with one's immediate manager as being the single most important factor linked with overall employee turnover.[26] First-line managers are frequently new to formal leadership roles, having previously been individual contributors themselves, and are preoccupied with learning to oversee a broad set of technical responsibilities in addition to managing people.

Under pressure to perform, managers may revert to the set of "go-to" people with whom they are most familiar, and shy away from proactively managing the diversity on their teams. This tendency can be unintentionally reinforced by a human resource department that provides a scary list of "don'ts" regarding protected classes of employees, sexual harassment, and/or discriminatory acts that could embarrass the organization and instantly derail a manager's career. Providing managers or supervisors with information and skill-building opportunities to leverage the diversity on their teams can get these junior leaders pointed in a more inclusive direction while tapping their energy and ambition. They may also need to know that someone is paying attention in order to keep the task of countering natural sources of bias front of mind. The presence of a dedicated inclusion and diversity function keeping track of targeted KPIs is correlated with higher promotion rates for women and minorities.[27]

Most first-line managers welcome a list of "do's" that they can safely engage in while avoiding the "don'ts," yet many have to generate this list on their own, if ever, through lengthy trial and error. Here is a set of recommendations for supervisors to begin to comprehend and tap the full capabilities of their team members. The list of acceptable areas of conversation varies considerably according to cultural and legal norms; we have kept it focused on professional topics.

Figure 10.6: Do's For First-Line Managers or Supervisors

- **Relationship-Building:** Make an effort to get to know each team member. Ask about:
    - **Professional interests:** *Please tell me about what you're most interested in doing or learning.*
    - **Prior experience:** *What kind of prior work experience do you have that would help me to understand your background?*
    - **Strengths and areas for improvement:** *What would you identify as your own greatest strengths and/or areas for improvement?*

- **Current challenges or concerns:** *Do you see any particular challenges or have any concerns about your current tasks?*

- **Motivation:** *What kind of work do you find most exciting? What do you like most about your current role and what would you like to do more or less of if we can arrange it?*

- **Career plans, aspirations:** *Do you have any thoughts about the next steps in your career? Is there anything you are currently doing that you would like to do more of or to learn about?*

- **Requests for support:** *How can I best support you? What can I do to be a better manager?*

- **Open-ended:** *What else would you like me to know about you? Is there anything else you would like to discuss?*

  Note: Questions about personal subjects—hobbies, health, family, etc.—are expected in some cultures, especially in informal settings, and are regarded as prying or even illegal in others.

- **Opportunities:** Provide all team members with equal opportunities to participate in activities and take on tasks that fit their capabilities, including meeting attendance, technical training, and project assignments.

- **Informal Contacts:** Include all team members in informal conversations and events—water-cooler conversations, company updates, social occasions, and so on.

- **Feedback:** Ensure that all team members receive performance feedback on a timely, even-handed basis. Make comments that are constructive, objective, concrete, and conducive to action.

- **Assessment:** Focus assessment on job performance relative to key objectives; be careful to check for possible forms of bias when stating observations.

C. Transition to Executive: The challenges that occur at the upper end of the talent pipeline come in a variety of forms, and many of these are cultural. Leaders who have performed well within the confines of a particular function, business unit, or country operation may one day find themselves being assessed for or placed in executive roles with a different, less familiar set of norms. The two examples that follow illustrate how the assessment process itself may require cultural calibration, and show sample adjustments that individuals need to make.

What's Wrong with the Brazilians?

The director of leadership development for a major organization was surprised by the failure rate of high-potential Brazilian candidates going through the firm's "assessment center" evaluation process for the next level of leadership. The candidates from Brazil, even those with otherwise stellar credentials, were only passing the battery of assessment center tests at a 20% rate, far lower than the 50% rate of their North American peers. Upon further investigation, it turned out that Brazilian candidates were receiving very low scores for critical competencies such as "clear and direct communication" and "results orientation." Still mystified by these outcomes, the head of leadership development decided to sit in on some of these assessments. She realized that the core problem was primarily cultural: "When the candidates from Brazil were asked a question, they would usually respond first with a story, and only later with an answer. It turned out that they felt this was a better way to get their point across that was also quite common in their country, but it earned them consistently low grades from our North American assessors. When we coached them to flip their communication around and start with the answer before telling the story, the assessment results changed in a hurry. Our candidates soon even started to coach North Americans coming to Brazil on how to alter their own communication styles to become more effective."

Executive Presence

Henry, an Asian manager in a Western company voiced his despair over the feedback he had received. "They're telling me I don't have executive presence. What does this mean? I've worked here for twenty years and have always received great performance reviews. Now I've finally worked my way up almost to the top and they're telling me that something is missing. Is it the clothes that I'm wearing?" he asked, pointing to his shirt and shoes that conveyed a flawless business-casual appearance suited to his industry. "Or is it the fact that I'm originally from Hong Kong and don't speak perfect English?"

Upon further examination, it turned out that a key point was the way Henry was communicating

> information. "Henry is too much in the weeds," was a common remark from the top executive team members. "He needs to be able to step back and give us the picture at the 30,000 foot level, and then dive into the details if we need that level of analysis." What Henry had thought was a reasonable and important level of detail for others on the team turned out to be too much information. They wanted to hear his big picture summary and then to be able to drill down as needed. Once Henry began to adjust his style and provide the right doses of information at the right times, switching nimbly between his strategic summary and a "deeper dive" set of numbers when requested, he was soon welcomed to the executive team. Several team members commented that they had misjudged his capabilities.

In both of these cases, individuals who were at the cusp of taking on executive roles found ways to increase their self-awareness and to adjust their actions through frame-shifting, or style-switching. These are key global leadership capabilities that help leaders deal with culturally conditioned approaches to areas such as communication or hierarchy, which are frequent sources of misunderstanding. Learning to serve as a "cultural guide" is also important, as this enables leaders to explain why things are done a particular way in a different cultural setting, thereby assisting others with frame-shifting as well.[28]

But new executive team members should not be the only ones who are adapting. Senior level teams get the best results when all of their members have gone through diversifying experiences of their own—serving in various functions, businesses, and geographies, for example—and are prepared to adjust to each other. It is naturally important to have certain core operating procedures, but these should not be allowed to blind a team to different perspectives or prospects for doing business. Instead of expecting new members to simply assimilate themselves to a dominant monocultural style, leadership team members with an agile mindset will deliberately engage them as a source of possible insights into cultural norms, best practices, or untapped markets.

Conclusion

Individual initiative is the most powerful driver of inclusion. There is no substitute for leaders at all levels who are willing to take up the cause of inclusion because they believe in its value, both for the business and for everyone involved. Such initiative can also be inspired and its effects multiplied by the organizational levers described above; the combination of individual initiative with supportive systems can produce a productive whirl of creativity and enthusiasm. People shape the culture in which they live, and are in turn shaped by it.

Of course there may be a degree of diversity or inclusiveness that is overwhelming to an organization, especially one that is unprepared. Diverse perspectives that are irreconcilable or poorly managed inhibit timely decision-making and fully aligned implementation; inclusion that is overly focused on satisfying every constituency and checking every box becomes detached from the business case. And providing equal access to challenging opportunities does not mean staffing projects with employees who are unqualified. There is no single, easy switch for turning on inclusion, or for adjusting the setting upward. Selecting which organizational levers to pull and when depends on the organization and the needs of the business.

Yet what is ultimately at stake with inclusive leadership is the capacity of an organization to renew itself.[29] No business model or pattern of success lasts forever, and many once-mighty companies, not to mention empires, have been relegated to the dustbin of history or are now visibly in decline. Organizations need to be able to change and grow, to reinvent themselves in the face of shifting circumstances. The term sustainability has become overused, but inclusive leaders who embrace new ideas, colleagues, and ways of serving customers can make their institutions uniquely sustainable. Inclusion is the price of vitality, an essential ingredient for building open, self-renewing systems.

Endnotes

1. Inclusive Leadership Trends

[1] The concept of "growth mindset" was coined by Carol Dweck of Stanford University based on her work with disadvantaged students. Although her studies have been criticized in academic circles as difficult to replicate, the growth mindset idea has subsequently been adopted by major corporations and consultancies. Dweck has published numerous works on this topic, including the book, *Mindset: How you can fulfill your potential*. Constable & Robinson Limited, 2012. For her TED Talk summary, "The Power of Believing That You Can Improve," see: https://www.ted.com/talks/carol_dweck_the_power_of_believing_that_you_can_improve?language=en
An irony of the growth mindset approach is that it overlaps with the process orientation for which Japanese companies became famous in the 1980's, often under the rubric of "continuous improvement." At that time many U.S. executives and academics were critical of this movement as insufficiently results-oriented, yet now it is embraced as a new path to achieving better results.

[2] Behavioral therapies are based on the premise that changing one's actions can have lasting effects. The early, often-criticized behavior modification techniques of B.F. Skinner, which linked specific behaviors with positive or negative reinforcement, have since been supplanted with a variety of therapeutic methods that are now standard approaches for treating mental health disorders, marital problems, and substance abuse.

[3] See, for example, Tinna Nielsen and Lisa Kepinski, *Inclusion Nudges Guidebook*, Edition 2, January 2016.

[4] "Emerging markets" is a problematic term, as the countries that fall under this rubric are at least as distinct from one another as they are similar. See, e.g., "Why 'emerging markets' is an outdated definition," *Financial Times*, August 4, 2015. https://www.weforum.org/agenda/2015/08/why-emerging-markets-is-an-outdated-definition/ Another suggestion has been to use the term "high-growth" markets, but not all so-called emerging markets are growing rapidly, if at all. In general it seems most accurate to refer to the characteristics of specific countries, so we will use the "emerging markets" label sparingly throughout this book.

[5] "The International Migration Report 2017." *United Nations Department of Economic and Social Affairs*, December 18, 2017. https://www.un.org/development/desa/publications/international-migration-report-2017.html. "The number of migrants as a fraction of the population residing in high-income countries rose from 9.6% in 2000 to 14% in 2017."

[6] Clifford Geertz, cited in, "Clifford Geertz: Work and Legacy." *Institute for Advanced Study*. https://www.ias.edu/clifford-geertz-work-and-legacy

[7] Romain Dillet, "French data protection watchdog fines Google $57 million under the GDPR." *TechCrunch*, February 2019. https://techcrunch.com/2019/01/21/french-data-protection-watchdog-fines-google-57-million-under-the-gdpr/

[8] Richard Dobbs, et al, "Urban world: The shifting global business landscape." *McKinsey Global Institute*, October 2013. https://www.mckinsey.com/featured-insights/urbanization/urban-world-the-shifting-global-business-landscape

[9] Rocío Lorenzo, Nicole Voigt, Miki Tsusaka, Matt Krentz, and Katie Abouzahr. "How Diverse Leadership Teams Boost Innovation." *Boston Consulting Group*, January 2018. https://www.bcg.com/en-us/publications/2018/how-diverse-leadership-teams-boost-innovation.aspx

[10] Sylvia Ann Hewlett, Melinda Marshall, and Laura Sherbin. "How Diversity Can Drive Innovation." *Harvard Business Review*, December 2013. The authors note the importance of both Inherent diversity, defined as the characteristics people are born with (e.g., gender, ethnicity, sexual orientation), and acquired diversity, or traits gained through experience (e.g., working in another country, selling products to people of a different gender).

[11] "High-Impact and Inclusion: Diversity Models and Findings." *Bersin by Deloitte*, 2017.

[12] McKinsey Analysis. "Delivering Through Diversity." January 2018.

[13] *Glassdoor*, 2014.

[14] "Creating Competitive Advantage Through Workforce Diversity." *Corporate Leadership Council*, 2012.

[15] SheForShield: Insure Women to better protect all." *IFC and AXA*, September 2015.

[16] John Kotter. *Corporate Culture and Performance*. Free Press, 2011.

2. Inclusive Leadership: Dealing with Difference

[1] "The Global Leader." *Corporate Leadership Council (CLC) Human Resources*, Corporate Executive Board, Executive Briefing, February 2012.

[2] William Maddux is interviewed in the video, "How to Stimulate Creativity? Go Live Abroad." *INSEAD*, 2009. https://www.youtube.com/watch?v=aKcu_ztYCtk&t=358s

[3] Nancy Adler. *International Dimensions of Organizational Behavior*, 4th Edition. SouthWestern, 2002, 263.

[4] Exodus 2:22 describes the birth of Gershom to Zipporah and Moses: "And she bore him a son, and he called his name Gershom: for he said, I have been a stranger in a strange land." (The Bible, American King James Version)

⁵Warren Bennis and Robert Thomas. "Crucibles of Leadership." *Harvard Business Review*, 2002.

⁶We prefer the term "cultural competence" over similar terms such as "cultural intelligence" because it strongly suggests not only awareness but also effective action.

⁷Ernest Gundling, Terry Hogan, and Karen Cvitkovich. *What is Global Leadership? 10 Key Behaviors that Define Successful Global Leaders*. Nicholas Brealey, 2011, 54–57.

⁸Ernest Gundling, Christie Caldwell, and Karen Cvitkovich. *Leading Across New Borders: How to Succeed as the Center Shifts*. Wiley & Sons, 2015, 85.

⁹Baldwin, James. *The Price of the Ticket: Collected Non-Fiction*, 1948-1985. St. Martin's Press, 1985.

3. Inclusive Behavior: Learning About Bias

¹Daniel Kahneman. *Thinking Fast and Slow*. Farrar, Straus and Giroux, 2013.

²Edward Hall. *The Silent Language*. Fawcett Publications, Inc., 1959, 39.

³See, e.g., Daniel Goleman, *Emotional Intelligence: Why it Can Matter More than IQ*. Bantam Books, 1995; and "What Makes a Leader?," *Harvard Business Review*, 1998.

4. Unconscious Bias on a Global Team

¹Nancy Adler. *International Dimensions of Organizational Behavior,* 4th Edition. SouthWestern, 2002, 145-146.

²Jeffrey Young. "Most Professors Think They're Above-Average Teachers. And That's a Problem." *EdSurge*, May 24, 2018. https://www.edsurge.com/news/2018-05-24-most-professors-think-they-re-above-average-teachers-and-that-s-a-problem

³Global Team Assessment - https://www.globesmart.com/global-team-assessment/

⁴See Appendix A, Team Launch: Foundations, in *Leading Across New Borders*. Ernest Gundling, Christie Caldwell, and Karen Cvitkovich. Wiley & Sons, 2015, 187–189.

⁵Edmondson, Amy. "Psychological Safety and Learning Behavior in Work Teams." *Administrative Science Quarterly*, 44(2), June 1, 1999.

⁶Abeer Dubey and Julia Rozovsky, People Analytics, Google; https://www.youtube.com/watch?v=KZlSq_Hf08M&list=PLORfsVTCrTYL47i_E2CrroChUPJ2J2K-8&index=2

⁷Reference: Parsi, Novid. *5 Leaders Who Are Disrupting Diversity*. SHRM, January 16, 2017.

[8] Factors related to how trust is perceived in a global team context are: qualifications, relationships, performance, expectations, and ethics. See Appendix A, Team Launch: Foundations, in *Leading Across New Borders*. Ernest Gundling, Christie Caldwell, and Karen Cvitkovich. Wiley & Sons, 2015, 187-189.

[9] In the popular movie, "Crazy Rich Asians," which is based in Singapore, a Singaporean friend of the female protagonist must be asked three times to attend a party for the rich and famous before saying yes. She turns down the first two requests in proper ritual style so as to appear modest, and also to ascertain that the request was a real invitation rather than just a polite gesture, before immediately agreeing to the third request. It turns out she was actually so eager to attend that she already had the party attire in the trunk of her car! Colleagues steeped in an interdependent, hierarchical, indirect cultural context may need to be asked to contribute more than once because they want to blend in, and they prefer to confirm that such a request was made out of a genuine desire for input.

[10] In the same movie, the statement by the male protagonist that "Yes, we're comfortable" is properly interpreted by his astounded girlfriend as meaning, "Yes, we're rich."

[11] "Astro Teller: Predict Failures before Beginning." *Stanford Technology Ventures Program*. https://www.youtube.com/watch?v=mIVVlr0B0FA

[12] Ernest Gundling, Terry Hogan, and Karen Cvitkovich. *What is Global Leadership? 10 Key Behaviors that Define Successful Global Leaders*. Nicholas Brealey, 2011. See chapters 3-4.

[13] Unconscious bias is similar in some respects to the advanced "Terminator" model that reconstitutes itself all too quickly even after being cleaved or shattered.

5. Inclusive Behaviors: Building Key Skills & Working Across Boundaries

[1] Adapted from Gardenswartz, Lee, and Anita Rowe. *Diverse Teams at Work: Capitalizing on the Power of Diversity*. ©Society for Human Resources Management, 2003 (used with permission).

[2] Many ancient societies distinguished, for instance, between warriors and farmers, and names like the English words "Smith" or "Miller" reflect craft-based identities such as blacksmithing or milling grain.

[3] Adapted from Ernest Gundling, Christie Caldwell, and Karen Cvitkovich, *Leading Across New Borders: How to Succeed as the Center Shifts*. Wiley & Sons, 2015, 92.

[4] Ernest Gundling and Anita Zanchettin, eds. *Global Diversity: Winning Customers and Engaging Employees within World Markets*. Nicholas Brealey, 2008.

6. Inclusive Behaviors: Becoming a Champion & Getting Results

[1] Adapted from Ernest Gundling, Terry Hogan, and Karen Cvitkovich, *Leading Across New Borders: How to Succeed as the Center Shifts*, p. 132

[2] Edward de Bono, *Six Thinking Hats: An Essential Approach to Business Management*. Little, Brown and Company, 1985.

[3] See Ernest Gundling, *Working GlobeSmart*. Davies-Black, 2003, 223-225. Nancy Adler refers to these three steps of team interaction as scope, representation, and process.

[4] Tom Kelley. *The Ten Faces of Innovation*. Doubleday, 2005.

[5] Ernest Gundling, Terry Hogan, and Karen Cvitkovich. *What is Global Leadership? 10 Key Behaviors that Define Successful Global Leaders*. Nicholas Brealey, 2011, 92.

[6] Ibid, 92-94.

7. Brain-Based Leadership: What's Missing?

[1] Jena McGregor. "The Business Brain in Close-up." *Bloomberg Businessweek*, July 22, 2007. https://www.bloomberg.com/news/articles/2007-07-22/the-business-brain-in-close-up

[2] Sharon Begley. "West Brain, East Brain: What a Difference Culture Makes." *Newsweek*, February 18, 2010. Begley is also the author of several books, including "The Emotional Life of Your Brain," and "Train Your Mind, Change Your Brain."

[3] Angela Gutchess, Robert Welsh, Aysecan Boduroglu, and Denise Park. "Cultural differences in neural function associated with object processing." *Cognitive, Affective, & Behavioral Neuroscience*, 2006, 102-9.

[4] Study by Jonathan Freeman et al. originally published in *Neuroimage*, Vol. 47, No. 1, 2009; also summarized in an article by Beth Azar, "Your Brain on Culture," *American Psychological Association*, November 2010, Vol 41, No. 10, that cites numerous advances in the field of "cultural neuroscience." Nalini Ambady is quoted as stating, "We see that what the brain finds rewarding reflects the values of the dominant culture. People can see the same stimulus but have completely different neural responses." See also, for example, Heejung Kim and Joni Sasaki, "Cultural Neuroscience: Biology of the Mind in Cultural Contexts," *Annual Review of Psychology*, Vol. 65:487-514, January 2014.

[5] "The first stage of ethnocentric thought is *denial*, in which people who are isolated from other cultures consciously ignore those other cultures' values. The final stage of ethnocentric orientations is *minimization*. People in the minimization stage focus only on personal similarities (e.g., physical, biological, philosophical), but do not legitimize other societies' broad cultural frameworks." Jingzhu Zhang. "Test Review: The Intercultural

Development Inventory Manual." *Journal of Psychoeducational Assessment*, Sage Publications, February 20, 2014. http://journals.sagepub.com/doi/abs/10.1177/0734282913505075?journalCode=jpaa

[6]The Intercultural Development Continuum was originally developed by Mitchell Hammer and Milton Bennett. It is now owned by IDI, LLC, which is a division of Hammer Holdings, Inc. See, https://idiinventory.com/publications/the-intercultural-development-continuum-idc.

8. Regional Inclusion Challenges

[1]Jonathan Woetzel, Anu Madgavkar, et al. "The power of parity: Advancing women's equality in Asia Pacific." *McKinsey & Company*, April 2018. https://www.mckinsey.com/featured-insights/gender-equality/the-power-of-parity-advancing-womens-equality-in-asia-pacific

[2]Dominic Abrams, et al, "Ageism in Europe and the UK." *European Research Group on Attitudes to Age* (EURAGE), 2011. https://core.ac.uk/download/pdf/10635079.pdf

[3]There is considerable dispute about definitions of tribalism, its current influence in Africa, and the role of colonial powers in shaping it. See, for example, Christine Mungai, "Pundits who decry 'tribalism' know nothing about real tribes." *The Washington Post*, January 30, 2019. Mungai notes that traditional tribes shared culturally sanctioned forms of intergroup conflict resolution, and that women often married outside of their original ethnic groups. https://www.washingtonpost.com/outlook/pundits-who-decry-tribalism-know-nothing-about-real-tribes/2019/01/29/8d14eb44-232f-11e9-90cd-dedb0c92dc17_story.html?utm_term=.bc894ed96e51;. For a different point of view, see for example Roger Cohen, "Tribalism Here, and There." *The New York Times*, March 10, 2008. https://www.nytimes.com/2008/03/10/opinion/10webcohen.html

[4]See, for example, "Ghana: Traders Association Protest Alleged Closure of 400 Nigerian-Owned Shops in Ghana." *Premium Times*, September 24, 2018. https://allafrica.com/stories/201809250016.html

[5]According to United Nations estimates, the population of Nigeria will exceed that of the U.S. by around mid-century.

[6]See, for example, "Probe rape claim against GBA boss – FIDA." *Ghana Web*, January 21, 2019. https://www.ghanaweb.com/GhanaHomePage/NewsArchive/Probe-rape-claim-againt-GBA-boss-FIDA-716832

[7]Salih Booker and Ari Rickman."The Future is Africa, and the United States is Not Prepared." *The Washington Post*, June 6, 2018. https://www.washingtonpost.com/news/democracy-post/wp/2018/06/09/the-future-is-african-and-the-united-states-is-not-prepared/?utm_term=.23b8e518649e

[8] Randolph Schmid, "Africans have world's greatest genetic variation." NBC News, April 30, 2009. http://www.nbcnews.com/id/30502963/ns/technology_and_science-science/t/africans-have-worlds-greatest-genetic-variation/#.XE4wYlVKjIU; Michael Campbell and Sarah Tishkoff, "African Genetic Diversity: Implications for Human Demographic History, Modern Human Origins, and Complex Disease Mapping." *U.S. National Library of Medicine, National Institutes of Health*, October 13, 2010. https://www.ncbi.nlm.nih.gov/pmc/articles/PMC2953791/

[9] *CIA World Factbook*, 2017.

[10] Richard Fuchs. "Germany is Not Shrinking." *DeutscheWelle*, February 2, 2017. https://www.dw.com/en/germany-is-not-shrinking/a-37415327

[11] Charley-Kai John, "Number of migrants in Germany hits record high." *Reuters World News*, April 12, 2018.

[12] Gregor Aisch, et al, "Some Colleges Have More Students From the Top 1 Percent Than the Bottom 60. Find Yours." *The New York Times*, January 18, 2017. https://www.nytimes.com/interactive/2017/01/18/upshot/some-colleges-have-more-students-from-the-top-1-percent-than-the-bottom-60.html

[13] Kimberle Crenshaw. "Why Intersectionality Can't Wait." *The Washington Post*, September 24, 2015. https://www.washingtonpost.com/news/in-theory/wp/2015/09/24/why-intersectionality-cant-wait/?utm_term=.835c71d620b8 "Intersectionality, then, was my attempt to make feminism, anti-racist activism, and anti-discrimination law do what I thought they should—highlight the multiple avenues through which racial and gender oppression were experienced so that the problems would be easier to discuss and understand."

Kimberle Crenshaw. "Mapping the Margins: Intersectionality, Identity Politics, and Violence Against Women of Color." *Stanford Law Review*, Vol. 43, No. 6 (Jul., 1991), 1241–1299;

"Where systems of race, gender and class domination converge, as they do in the experiences of battered women of color, intervention strategies based solely on the experiences of women who do not share the same class or race backgrounds will be of limited help to women who because of race and class face different obstacles."

[14] David Pollock, Ruth Von Reken, and Michael Pollock. *Third Culture Kids: Growing Up Among Worlds*. Third Edition, Nicholas Brealey, 2017.

[15] Based on experiences recorded by Julia Sloan.

9. Inclusive Leadership Development

[1] In contrast, a highly anticipated crisis was Y2K, which turned out to be a relatively minor event in part because companies planned ahead to blunt its impact (millennials may have to look this up).

²Pagan Kennedy. "William Gibson's Future is Now." *The New York Times*, January 13, 2012. https://www.nytimes.com/2012/01/15/books/review/distrust-that-particular-flavor-by-william-gibson-book-review.html

³Simone Ritter, Rodica Damian, Dean Simonton, et al. "Diversifying Experiences Enhance Cognitive Flexibility." *Journal of Experimental Social Psychology*, February 21, 2012.

⁴Ibid.

⁵See, for example, Ernest Gundling, Terry Hogan, and Karen Cvitkovich. *What is Global Leadership? 10 Key Behaviors that Define Successful Global Leaders*. Nicholas Brealey, 2011; Paula Caligiuri, *Cultural Agility: Building a Pipeline of Successful Global Professionals*. Jossey-Bass, 2014; Andy Molinsky. *Global Dexterity: How to Adapt Your Behavior Across Cultures without Losing Yourself in the Process*. Harvard Business Review Press, 2013.

⁶Ritter, Damian, and Simonton, Ibid.

⁷Nancy Adler. *International Dimensions of Organizational Behavior*, 4th Edition. SouthWestern, 2002, 263.

⁸Herminia Ibarra. "The Authenticity Paradox." *Harvard Business Review*, January–February 2015.

⁹ Rick Hanson describes this process in a personal development context using his HEAL model. Rick Hanson. *Hardwiring Happiness: The New Brain Science of Contentment, Calm, and Confidence*. Harmony, 2016.

¹⁰See, for example, David Drake, *Narrative Coaching*. CNC Press, 2015.

¹¹Lecture by Professor Albert Hastorf, Stanford University Department of Psychology.

10. Five Organizational Levers

¹Marshall Goldsmith. *What Got You Here Won't Get You There*. Hachette Books, 2007.

²Excerpted and adapted from *5 Leaders Who Are Disrupting Diversity*, by Novid Parsi. ©Society for Human Resource Management, January 16, 2017 (used with permission). Photo by Daniel Berman.

³In the U.S., this is commonly called the "Rooney Rule," a practice in professional football that requires interviewing at least one minority candidate for open coaching positions.

⁴Excerpted and adapted from *5 Leaders Who Are Disrupting Diversity*, by Novid Parsi. ©Society for Human Resource Management, January 16, 2017 (used with permission). Photo by Jose Luis Stephens.

[5] Rocío Lorenzo, Nicole Voigt, Miki Tsusaka, Matt Krentz, and Katie Abouzahr. "How Diverse Leadership Teams Boost Innovation." *Boston Consulting Group*, January 2018. https://www.bcg.com/en-us/publications/2018/how-diverse-leadership-teams-boost-innovation.aspx

[6] An interview with Iris Bohnet by Gardiner Morse, "Designing a Bias-Free Organization." *Harvard Business Review*, July–August 2016.

[7] Frank Dobbin and Alexandra Kalev. "Why Diversity Programs Fail." *Harvard Business Review*, July–August 2016. The authors note a significant positive correlation between the presence of mentoring programs and higher numbers of minorities in management roles.

[8] Catherine Tinsley and Robert Ely. "What Most People Get Wrong about Men and Women." *Harvard Business Review*, May–June 2018.

[9] See, for example, Lisa Burrell, "We Just Can't Handle Diversity." *Harvard Business Review*, July–August 2016.

[10] The Thomson Reuters Diversity and Inclusion Rating is an example of a broad index that tracks 24 separate items in four major categories: Diversity, Inclusion, News and Controversies, and People Development. It draws upon open information sources for publicly listed companies. https://www.refinitiv.com/content/dam/gl/en/documents/methodology/diversity-inclusion-rating-methodology.pdf

[11] Ashleigh Shelby Rosette of Duke University as quoted by Lisa Burrell in "We Just Can't Handle Diversity." *Harvard Business Review*, July–August 2016.

[12] Tomas Chamorro-Premuzic. "Does Diversity Actually Increase Creativity?" *Harvard Business Review*, June 28, 2017.

[13] "Of the six dimensions of diversity we considered, all showed a correlation with innovation. But he most significant gains came from changing the makeup of the leadership team in terms of the national origin of executives, range of industry backgrounds, gender balance, and career paths." Rocío Lorenzo, Nicole Voigt, Miki Tsusaka, Matt Krentz, and Katie Abouzahr. "How Diverse Leadership Teams Boost Innovation." *Boston Consulting Group*, January 2018. https://www.bcg.com/en-us/publications/2018/how-diverse-leadership-teams-boost-innovation.aspx

[14] See, for example, Roscoe Balter, Joy Chow, and Yin Jin, "What Diversity Metrics are Best Used to Track and Improve Employee Diversity." Cornell University Industrial and Labor Relations School, *DigitalCommons@ILR*, Spring 2014. https://digitalcommons.ilr.cornell.edu/cgi/viewcontent.cgi?referer=http://www.societyfordiversity.org/diversity-metrics-measurement-where-should-senior-execs-begin/&httpsredir=1&article=1063&context=student; also, see Leah Smiley, "5 Must-Have Metrics for Diversity & Inclusion to Prove ROI." *The Society for Diversity*, October 10 2016. http://www.societyfordiversity.org/5-must-have-metrics-for-diversity-inclusion-to-prove-roi

[15] Robert Austin and Gary Pisano. "Neurodiversity as a Competitive Advantage." *Harvard Business Review*, May–June 2017.

[16] For more information about the Inclusive Behaviors Inventory: https://www.globesmart.com/inclusive-behaviors-inventory/

[17] Average dimension ranking from lowest to highest was as follows: Working Across Boundaries, Getting Results, Becoming a Champion, Learning About Bias, and Building Key Skills.

[18] Frank Dobbin and Alexandra Kalev. "Why Diversity Programs Fail." H*arvard Business Review*, July–August 2016.

[19] Rocío Lorenzo, Nicole Voigt, Miki Tsusaka, Matt Krentz, and Katie Abouzahr. "How Diverse Leadership Teams Boost Innovation." *Boston Consulting Group*, January 2018. https://www.bcg.com/en-us/publications/2018/how-diverse-leadership-teams-boost-innovation.aspx

[20] The ways that people react to directives are of course shaped by national and organizational cultures. Even very hierarchical cultures often have mechanisms for soliciting input or providing a measure of autonomy in the implementation process.

[21] An interview with Iris Bohnet by Gardiner Morse. "Designing a Bias-Free Organization." *Harvard Business Review*, July–August 2016.

[22] "Choice architecture" is one term for this type of approach to mitigating deeply-ingrained biases: "The idea is to deliberately structure how you present information and options. You don't take away individuals' right to decide or tell them what they should do. You just make it easier for them to reach more-rational decisions." Lisa Burrell. "We Just Can't Handle Diversity." *Harvard Business Review,* July–August 2016.

[23] Joan Williams and Marina Multhaup. "For Women and Minorities to Get Ahead, Managers Must Assign Work Fairly." *Harvard Business Review*, March 5, 2018.

[24] See, for example, Matt Krentz , "Survey: What Diversity and Inclusion Policies Do Employees Actually Want?" *Harvard Business Review*, March 5, 2019. Also, see Tracy Brower on the topic of work-life fulfillment in "We Need to Stop Striving for Work-Life Balance. Here's Why." *Fast Company*, February 16, 2019. https://www.fastcompany.com/90308095/why-you-should-stop-trying-to-achieve-work-life-balance

[25] See, e.g., Kevin Sneader and Lareina Yee, "One is the loneliest number." *McKinsey Quarterly*, January 2019. https://www.mckinsey.com/featured-insights/gender-equality/one-is-the-loneliest-number. "When women find themselves alone in a group of men… they are far more likely than others to have their judgment questioned than women working in a more balanced environment (49 percent versus 32 percent), to be mistaken for someone more junior (35 percent versus 15 percent), and to be subjected to unprofessional and demeaning remarks (24 percent versus 14 percent). If they are treated like this, no wonder they get overlooked for promotion."

[26] Marcus Buckingham. *First, Break All The Rules: What the World's Greatest Managers Do Differently*. Gallup Press, 2016.

[27] Frank Dobbin and Alexandra Kalev. "Why Diversity Programs Fail." *Harvard Business Review*, July–August 2016. "Diversity managers sometimes put ineffective programs in place but have a positive impact overall —in part because managers know someone might ask them about their hiring and promotion decisions."

[28] See Ernest Gundling, Terry Hogan, and Karen Cvitkovich. *What is Global Leadership? 10 Key Behaviors that Define Successful Global Leaders*. Nicholas Brealey, 2011, chapters 3–4.

[29] Renewal is a favorite theme, for example, of Satya Nadella, Microsoft's third-generation CEO, who has been lauded for his efforts to change the organization in response to market trends. Originally born in Hyderabad, India, Nadella is now the head of a company founded in the Pacific Northwest region of the U.S. with over 130,000 employees worldwide. Microsoft faces a classic renewal challenge as the personal computer market fades and new business opportunities such as cloud computing are fiercely contested.

Bibliography

Adler, Nancy. *International Dimensions of Organizational Behavior*. 4th ed. Mason, OH: Thomson South-Western, 2002.

Aisch, Gregor, Larry Buchanan, Amanda Cox and Kevin Quealy. "Some Colleges Have More Students From the Top 1 Percent Than the Bottom 60. Find Yours." *The New York Times*, January 18, 2017.

Freeman, Jonathan B., Nicholas O. Rule, Reginald B. Adams, Jr., and Nalini Ambady. "Culture shapes a mesolimbic response to signals of dominance and subordination that associates with behavior" *NeuroImage*, 47(1), 353–359, August 1, 2009.

Austin, Robert, and Gary Pisano. "Neurodiversity as a Competitive Advantage." *Harvard Business Review*, May-June 2017.

Azar, Beth. "Your Brain on Culture." *American Psychological Association*, 41(10), November 2010.

Baldwin, James. *The Price of the Ticket: Collected Non-Fiction*, 1948–1985. New York: St. Martin's Press, 1985.

Balter, Roscoe, Joy Chow, and Yin Jin. "What Diversity Metrics are Best Used to Track and Improve Employee Diversity." *DigitalCommons@ILR*. Cornell University Industrial and Labor Relations School, Spring 2014.

Begley, Sharon. "West Brain, East Brain: What a Difference Culture Makes." *Newsweek*, February 18, 2010.

Bennis, Warren, and Robert Thomas. "Crucibles of Leadership." *Harvard Business Review*, 2002.

Bersin by Deloitte. "High-Impact and Inclusion: Diversity Models and Findings." 2017.

Booker, Salih, and Ari Rickman. "The Future is Africa, and the United States is Not Prepared." *The Washington Post*, June 6, 2018.

Brower, Tracy. "We Need to Stop Striving for Work-Life Balance. Here's Why." *Fast Company*, February 16, 2019.

Buckingham, Marcus. *First, Break All The Rules: What the World's Greatest Managers Do Differently*. Gallup Press, 2016.

Burrell, Lisa. "We Just Can't Handle Diversity." *Harvard Business Review*, July–August 2016.

Caligiuri, Paula. *Cultural Agility: Building a Pipeline of Successful Global Professionals*. San Francisco: Jossey-Bass, 2014.

Campbell, Michael C., and Sarah A. Tishkoff. "African Genetic Diversity: Implications for Human Demographic History, Modern Human Origins, and Complex Disease Mapping." *Annual Review of Genomics and Human Genetics*, Vol. 9, 403-433, September 22, 2008.

Chamorro-Premuzic, Tomas. "Does Diversity Actually Increase Creativity?" *Harvard Business Review*, June 28, 2017.

Cho, Karen. "How to Stimulate Creativity? Go Live Abroad." *INSEAD Knowledge*, June 12, 2009.

Cohen, Roger. "Tribalism Here, and There." *The New York Times*, March 10, 2008.

Corporate Leadership Council. "Creating Competitive Advantage Through Workforce Diversity." 2012.

Corporate Leadership Council. "The Global Leader." Corporate Executive Board report, 2012.

Crenshaw, Kimberle. "Mapping the Margins: Intersectionality, Identity Politics, and Violence Against Women of Color." *Stanford Law Review*, 43 (6), July 1991.

Crenshaw, Kimberle. "Why Intersectionality Can't Wait." *The Washington Post*, September 24, 2015.

de Bono, Edward. *Six Thinking Hats: An Essential Approach to Business Management*. Boston: Little, Brown and Company, 1985.

Dobbin, Frank, and Alexandra Kalev. "Why Diversity Programs Fail." *Harvard Business Review*, July–August 2016.

Dobbs, Richard, et al. "Urban world: The shifting global business landscape." *McKinsey Global Institute*, October 2013.

David Drake, *Narrative Coaching: Bringing Our New Stories to Life*. Petaluma, CA: CNC Press, 2015.

Edmondson, Amy. "Psychological Safety and Learning Behavior in Work Teams." *Administrative Science Quarterly*, 44(2), June 1, 1999.

Financial Times. "Why 'emerging markets' is an outdated definition." August 4, 2015.

Fuchs, Richard. "Germany is Not Shrinking." *DeutscheWelle*, February 2, 2017.

Gardenswartz, Lee, and Anita Rowe. "Diverse Teams at Work: Capitalizing on the Power of Diversity." *Society for Human Resource Management*, 2003.

Ghana Web. "Probe rape claim against GBA boss – FIDA." January 21, 2019.

Goldsmith, Marshall. *What Got You Here Won't Get You There*. New York: Hyperion, 2007.

Goleman, Daniel. *Emotional Intelligence: Why it Can Matter More than IQ*. New York: Bantam Books, 1995.

Goleman, Daniel. "What Makes a Leader?" *Harvard Business Review*, January 2004.

Gundling, Ernest, and Anita Zanchettin, eds. *Global Diversity: Winning Customers and Engaging Employees within World Markets*. Boston & London: Nicholas Brealey, 2008.

Gundling, Ernest, Christie Caldwell, and Karen Cvitkovich. *Leading Across New Borders: How to Succeed as the Center Shifts*. Hoboken, NJ: Wiley & Sons, 2015.

Gundling, Ernest, Terry Hogan, and Karen Cvitkovich. *What is Global Leadership? 10 Key Behaviors that Define Successful Global Leaders*. Boston & London: Nicholas Brealey, 2011.

Gundling, Ernest. *Working GlobeSmart: 12 People Skills for Doing Business Across Borders*. Boston & London: Davies-Black, 2003.

Gutchess, Angela H., Robert C. Welsh, Aysecan Boduroglu, and Denise Park. "Cultural differences in neural function associated with object processing." *Cognitive, Affective, & Behavioral Neuroscience*, 6(2), 102–109, 2006.

Hall, Edward. *The Silent Language*. Greenwich, CT: Fawcett Publications, Inc., 1959.

Hanson, Rick. Hardwiring Happiness: *The New Brain Science of Contentment, Calm, and Confidence*. New York: Harmony, 2016.

Hewlett, Sylvia Ann, Melinda Marshall, and Laura Sherbin. "How Diversity Can Drive Innovation." *Harvard Business Review*, December 2013.

Ibarra, Herminia. "The Authenticity Paradox." *Harvard Business Review*, January–February 2015.

Institute for Advanced Study. "Clifford Geertz: Work and Legacy." No date.

International Finance Corporation and AXA Group. "SheForShield: Insure Women to better protect all." September 2015.

John, Charley-Kai. "Number of migrants in Germany hits record high." *Reuters World News*, April 12, 2018.

Kahneman, Daniel. *Thinking Fast and Slow*. New York: Farrar, Straus and Giroux, 2013.

Kelley, Tom. *The Ten Faces of Innovation*. New York: Doubleday, 2005.

Kennedy, Pagan. "William Gibson's Future is Now." *New York Times*, January 13, 2012.

Kim, Heejung, and Joni Sasaki. "Cultural Neuroscience: Biology of the Mind in Cultural Contexts." *Annual Review of Psychology*, Vol. 65, 487–514, January 2014.

Kimsey-House, Henry. Kimsey-House, Karen et al. *Co-Active Coaching*, Fourth Edition. Boston: Nicholas Brealey, 2018.

Kotter, John. *Corporate Culture and Performance*. New York: Free Press, 2011.

Kotter, John. *Leading Change*. Boston: Harvard Business Review Press, 2012.

Krentz, Matt. "Survey: What Diversity and Inclusion Policies Do Employees Actually Want?" *Harvard Business Review*, March 5, 2019.

Lorenzo, Rocío, Nicole Voigt, Miki Tsusaka, Matt Krentz, and Katie Abouzahr. "How Diverse Leadership Teams Boost Innovation." *Boston Consulting Group*, January 2018.

MacDonald, Heather. *The Diversity Delusion: How Race and Gender Pandering Corrupt the University and Undermine our Culture*. New York: St. Martin's Press, 2018.

McGregor, Jena. "The Business Brain in Close-up." *Bloomberg Businessweek*, July 22, 2007.

McKinsey Analysis. "Delivering Through Diversity." January 2018.

Molinsky, Andy. *Global Dexterity: How to Adapt Your Behavior Across Cultures without Losing Yourself in the Process*. Boston: Harvard Business Review Press, 2013.

Morse, Gardiner. Interview with Iris Bohnet. "Designing a Bias-Free Organization." *Harvard Business Review*, July–August 2016.

Mungai, Christine. "Pundits who decry 'tribalism' know nothing about real tribes." *The Washington Post*, January 30, 2019.

Nadella, Satya. *Hit Refresh: The Quest to Rediscover Microsoft's Soul and Imagine a Better Future for Everyone*. New York: HarperCollins, 2017.

Nielsen, Tinna, and Lisa Kepinski. *Inclusion Nudges Guidebook*. Edition 2, January 2016.

Pollock, David C., Ruth E. Von Reken, and Michael V. Pollock. *Third Culture Kids: Growing Up Among Worlds*, Third Edition. Boston & London: Nicholas Brealey, 2017.

Premium Times. "Ghana: Traders Association Protest Alleged Closure of 400 Nigerian-Owned Shops in Ghana." September 24, 2018.

Ritter, Simone, Rodica Damian, Dean Simonton, et al. "Diversifying Experiences Enhance Cognitive Flexibility." *Journal of Experimental Social Psychology*, February 21, 2012.

Rock, David. *Your Brain at Work*. New York: HarperCollins, 2009.

Ross, Howard. *Reinventing Diversity: Transforming Organizational Community to Strengthen People, Purpose, and Performance*. Lanham, Maryland: Rowman and Littlefield, 2011.

Ross, Howard. *Everyday Bias: Identifying and Navigating Unconscious Judgments in Our Daily Lives*. Lanham, Maryland: Rowman and Littlefield, 2014.

Schmid, Randolph E. "Africans have world's greatest genetic variation." *Science on NBCNews.com*, April 30, 2009.

Smiley, Leah. "5 Must-Have Metrics for Diversity & Inclusion to Prove ROI." *The Society for Diversity*, October 10, 2016.

Sneader, Kevin, and Lareina Yee. "One is the loneliest number." *McKinsey Quarterly*, January 2019.

Tapia, Andrés. *The Inclusion Paradox: The Post-Obama Era and the Transformation of Global Diversity*, Third Edition. Korn Ferry Institute, 2016.

The World Factbook. Washington, DC: Central Intelligence Agency, 2017.

Thomson Reuters. "Thomson Reuters Diversity and Inclusion Rating." 2018.

Tinsley, Catherine, and Robert Ely. "What Most People Get Wrong about Men and Women." *Harvard Business Review*, May–June 2018.

United Nations Department of Economic and Social Affairs. "The International Migration Report 2017." December 18, 2017.

Williams, Joan, and Marina Multhaup. "For Women and Minorities to Get Ahead, Managers Must Assign Work Fairly." *Harvard Business Review*, March 5, 2018.

Woetzel, Jonathan. Anu Madgavkar et al. "The power of parity: Advancing women's equality in Asia Pacific." *McKinsey & Company*, April 2018.

Young, Jeffrey. "Most Professors Think They're Above-Average Teachers. And That's a Problem." *EdSurge*, May 24, 2018.

Zhang, Jingzhu. "Test Review: The Intercultural Development Inventory Manual." *Journal of Psychoeducational Assessment*, February 20, 2014.

Resources

Books

- *Global Diversity: Winning Customers and Engaging Employees within World Markets* presents the key cultural variables relevant in eight major markets. The business impact of each unique set of diversity variables is explored and recommendations are provided for developing employees and realizing local market opportunities.

- *Leading Across New Borders: How to Succeed as the Center Shifts* explores new imperatives that will help global leaders better understand and navigate across cultures, markets, and management differences.

Quick Guides

- **Quick Guide to Unconscious Bias**
  http://tiny.cc/UBQuickGuide

- **Analyzing Your Talent Life Cycle for Inclusion**
  http://tiny.cc/TalentLifeCycle

- **6 Tips for an Inclusive Recruitment Strategy**
  http://tiny.cc/InclusiveRecruitment

- **Quick Guide to Managing Inclusively**
  http://tiny.cc/InclusiveManagement

- **Tips to Prevent Bias on Global Teams**
  http://tiny.cc/TeamBias

Assessments and Tools

- **GlobeSmart Profile**—Work smarter, faster, and more collaboratively. Create a common vocabulary to address previously hidden biases. Understanding and adapting to work style differences are key steps toward more inclusive leadership.
www.globesmart.com

- **Inclusive Behaviors Inventory**—Measure the inclusivity of people in your organization. You'll get actionable advice and strategies based on the assessment scores. A 360 version is available for executives or for leadership teams.
www.globesmart.com/inclusive-behaviors-inventory

- **Global Team Assessment**— Gather feedback and discover team strengths, weaknesses, and key areas for development. When your team members focus together on how to improve their performance, your meetings are better, conflict is resolved faster, and shared objectives are more readily achieved.
www.globesmart.com/global-team-assessment

- **Global Competencies Inventory**—Assess your organization's global leadership capabilities with this statistically robust tool. Inventory results can be used as part of a candidate selection process and for targeted training and coaching.
www.globesmart.com/global-competencies-inventory

About The Authors

Ernest Gundling, Ph.D., is a co-founder and managing partner of Aperian Global. He assists clients in building strategic global approaches to leadership development, inclusion and diversity, and cross-border business relationships. He has lived and traveled extensively in Asia, Europe, Latin America, and the Middle East, including six years as an expatriate in Japan. A frequent keynote speaker and the author of five previous books—including *What is Global Leadership?*, *Global Diversity*, and *Leading Across New Borders*—he has also served for twenty-five years as a Lecturer at the Haas School of Business at the University of California, Berkeley.

• • •

Cheryl Williams, Ph.D., is a highly regarded subject matter expert on global workforce inclusion, diversity matters, cultural competency and leadership across boundaries. She spent over twenty-five years in leadership roles in the entertainment and high technology industries where she managed employee education and training, recruitment, staffing, internal communications, employee relations, and community relations. She has worked extensively in over fifty countries, and serves as Professor Emeritus at Concordia University, Irvine, California.

About Aperian Global

Aperian Global has provided consulting, training, and online learning tools to 40% of the Global Fortune 100. Aperian Global's employees are dedicated to helping clients work effectively across boundaries, both at home and abroad. The company provides scalable resources for building practical skills and knowledge that help individuals and organizations thrive in an increasingly diverse business landscape.

Aperian Global specializes in research-based inclusion practices—impactful in domestic work environments and adaptable to different world regions—along with strategic global mobility support and holistic cultural competence learning solutions. *GlobeSmart,* the company's flagship online tool, has had more than one million users, and its work-style profile provides a way for team members to compare their styles and adjust to each other. The *Inclusive Behaviors Inventory,* available in both self-assessment and 360 versions, is also part of the *GlobeSmart* platform's assessment suite.

Aperian Global's products and services empower leaders at all levels to work in an inclusive way, engaging partners, colleagues, and employees from any background to deliver results through high-performance teamwork.

Founded in 1990, Aperian Global has offices in Bangalore, Boston, Kolding, Oakland, Paris, Raleigh, Shanghai, and Singapore, and staff and consultants on the ground in over 80 locations worldwide.

For more information, visit www.aperianglobal.com.

Made in the USA
Middletown, DE
30 July 2020